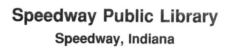

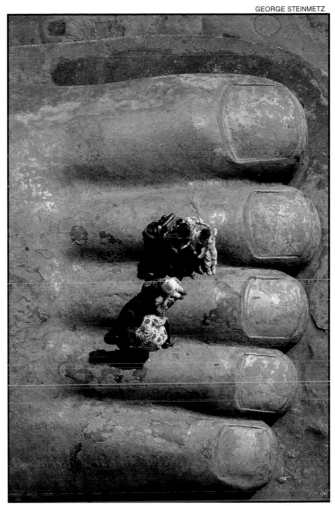

*In Leshan, China, tourists and pilgrims rest on a giant Buddha's toes.*

# Great Journeys

# of the World

Prepared by
The Book Division
National Geographic Society
Washington, D.C.

# Great Journeys of the World

*Contributing Authors*

Elisabeth B. Booz
Patrick R. Booz
Thurston Clarke
Ron Fisher
Cynthia Russ Ramsay

*Contributing Photographers*

**Jodi Cobb,** *National Geographic Photographer*
**Sarah Leen**
**Maggie Steber**
**George Steinmetz**

*Published by*
The National Geographic Society

**Reg Murphy,** *President and Chief Executive Officer*
**Gilbert M. Grosvenor,** *Chairman of the Board*
**Nina D. Hoffman,** *Senior Vice President*

*Prepared by*
The Book Division

**William R. Gray,** *Vice President and Director*
**Charles Kogod,** *Assistant Director*
**Barbara A. Payne,** *Editorial Director*

**Staff for this book**

Jane H. Buxton,
 *Managing Editor*
Greta Arnold,
 *Illustrations Editor*
Cinda Rose,
 *Art Director*
Elisabeth B. Booz,
Victoria Cooper,
Susan A. Franques,
 *Researchers*
Martha C. Christian,
Mary B. Dickinson,
 *Consulting Editors*

Carl Mehler,
 *Map Editor*
Margaret Deane Gray,
Joseph F. Ochlak,
Louis J. Spirito,
 *Map Researchers*

James Huckenpahler,
 *Map Production*
Tibor G. Tóth,
 *Map Relief*

Richard S. Wain,
 *Production Project Manager*
Lewis R. Bassford,
 *Production*

Jennifer L. Burke,
Karen Dufort Sligh,
 *Illustrations Assistants*
Kevin G. Craig,
Dale M. Herring,
Sandra F. Lotterman,
Peggy J. Oxford,
 *Staff Assistants*

Manufacturing and Quality
 Management

George V. White,
 *Director*
John T. Dunn,
 *Associate Director*
Vincent P. Ryan,
 *Manager*

Elisabeth MacRae-Bobynskyj,
 *Indexer*

*Sunrise defines an acacia tree, essential
shade-giver of East Africa's plains.
PRECEDING PAGES: Spewing flames,
a Rajasthani fire-eater performs
for a folk music and dance evening
at Jaipur's Nahargarh Fort.
FOLLOWING PAGES: Water taxi's mirror
vignettes Santa Maria della Salute
across Venice's Basin of San Marco
from San Giorgio Maggiore.*

BOYD NORTON
PRECEDING PAGES: SARAH LEEN
FOLLOWING PAGES: NGS PHOTOGRAPHER JODI COBB

# Contents

Crossing Europe on the

# Orient

# Express

by Ron Fisher

Photographs by Jodi Cobb,

National Geographic Photographer,

and Maggie Steber

*New incarnation of the fabled* Orient Express *glides through Paris on its Boulogne-Venice run.*

*The Eiffel Tower symbolizes the glamour and romance of Paris, the City of Light.*

*I*t's April in Paris, but the City of Light is buried in cold, gray drizzle. Tourists at the Arc de Triomphe huddle together, shivering, puzzling over the French inscriptions, as a gusty wind sweeps down the Champs-Elysées, spattering them with rain.

At the drafty Gare de l'Est, the giant train station that looks eastward from Paris toward Germany and beyond, I'm having a croissant and coffee. I'm waiting for a train. I have my sights set on sunnier climes: the Balkans and beyond, Budapest and Bucharest, the western fringe of Asia, the storied stones of old Constantinople. I'm going by train from Paris to Istanbul, following the 1883 inaugural route of the *Train Express d'Orient*.

The very name conjures romance. For many years the *Orient Express* was *the* train to take across Europe, the ultimate in elegance and luxury, where you could hobnob with high society, rub elbows with royalty and film stars, and imagine yourself in the company of international jewel thieves or spies. The train impressed passengers with rich carpeting, damask draperies, teak and mahogany paneling, armchairs covered in soft Spanish leather, and fine cuisine.

It was the dream of a Belgian entrepreneur named Georges Nagelmackers. He gave his company a name that rolls invitingly off the tongue: Compagnie Internationale des Wagons-Lits.

Contrary to popular belief, the *Orient Express* was never one single line of track. There were a number of routes to the East, luxury services initiated in the late 19th and early 20th centuries. And in 1906, the Simplon Tunnel—then the world's longest railway tunnel at 12½ miles—opened in the Alps, linking Switzerland and Italy. In 1919 the *Orient Express* began a service called "Simplon-*Orient-Express*" using this route.

The *Orient Express* between Paris and Istanbul made its last regular run in 1977 after a couple of decades of declining ridership, caused largely by air travel. But the tracks are still there, and trains run on them, and it's perfectly possible to duplicate the 1,800 miles of the *Orient Express*'s 1883 inaugural run.

The train I board in Paris is new, squeaky clean, and starts on time to the minute. I'm riding backward, which always makes me feel as if I'm going south. I'm in a compartment with a sliding glass door. Two comfortable seats, each built to accommodate three people, face each other.

Paul Theroux, in *The Great Railway Bazaar*, wrote: "I sought trains; I found passengers." Similarly, what I'll remember from the trip are the people I encounter along the way.

Two French businessmen share the compartment with me. They have long, pale faces and thin hands. Our lack of a mutual language eliminates small talk. One lays his briefcase on his lap and uses it as a table as he works for 15 minutes on his glasses, tightening screws with tiny jewelers' tools and polishing the lenses with a soft cloth, which he folds fastidiously when he is finished. They talk quietly together, laughing now and then. Their liquid language sounds like singing.

One has a newspaper and I glimpse a photo of a badly damaged building and a headline: *Dévastation dans Oklahoma*....

We pass through the industrial outskirts and suburbs of Paris. Mist rises from a quiet river, where barges make gentle

*11*

**VENICE SIMPLON ORIENT-EXPRESS**

*T*he Orient Express *made rail history in 1883 by inaugurating the first trans-European service, an 1,800-mile journey between Paris and Constantinople (now Istanbul). By its last run in 1977 it had become an almost mythical symbol of sophisticated elegance. Since the opening of Eastern Europe, the same rails carry passengers by regular trains across seven*

PERA PALAS

ORIENT EXPRESS BAR

WALES

ENGLAND

London ★

Folkestone

*North Sea*

NETHERLANDS

POLAND

*English Channel*

Boulogne

BELGIUM

LUX.

*Rhine*

GERMANY

Prague ★

CZECH REPUBLIC

SLOVAKIA

Paris ★

Epernay

Pogny

Nancy

*Seine*

Strasbourg

*Neckar R.*

Stuttgart

Göppingen

*Danube*

Ulm

Augsburg

Munich

Endorf

Vienna ★

Hegyeshalom

Budapest ★

Basel

ARLBERG TUNNEL

Salzburg

AUSTRIA

HUNGARY

Chişineu-Criş

Szeged

Zürich

FRANCE

SWITZ.

LIECH.

Innsbruck

*Inn*

A  L  P  S

SLOVENIA

CROATIA

SIMPLON TUNNEL

A  L

Verona

Venice

BOSNIA & HERZG.

I  T  A  L  Y

*Adriatic Sea*

YUG.

ALBANIA

*Mediterranean Sea*

À CARTE

E DEJEUNER

countries. *The restored*
*Venice Simplon-Orient-*
*Express resumed the*
*tradition of fine service*
*in 1982 on a 1,065-mile*
*route between London*
*and Venice, a luxurious*
*journey of 32 hours.*

ORIENT-EXPRESS

May 7

Jane –

I bounced off all four
walls of my compartment
last night getting into my
tux – but I was the prettiest
one on the train.

See you soon.

Rose

Hotel Sacher

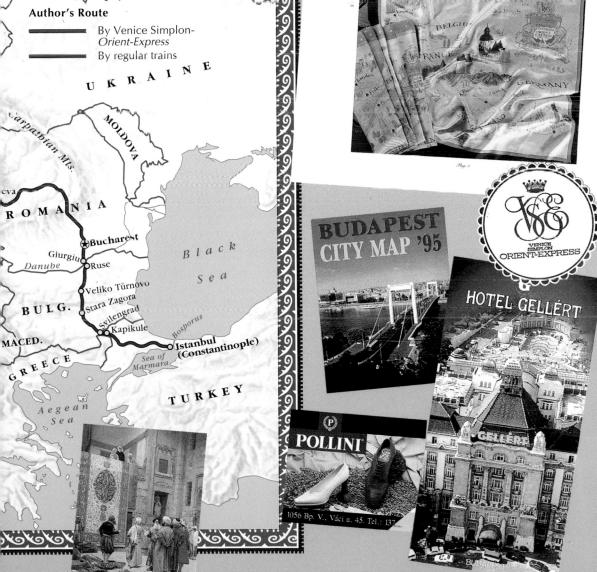

**Author's Route**

By Venice Simplon-
*Orient-Express*
By regular trains

0 — 200 mi
0 — 300 km

BELARUS

RUSSIA

UKRAINE

MOLDOVA

Carpathian Mts.

cva

ROMANIA

Bucharest

Giurgiu
Danube
Ruse

Veliko Tŭrnovo

Stara Zagora

BULG.

Svilengrad

Kapikule

MACED.

GREECE

Aegean
Sea

Black
Sea

Bosporus

Istanbul
(Constantinople)

Sea of
Marmara

TURKEY

BUDAPEST
CITY MAP '95

VENICE
SIMPLON
ORIENT-EXPRESS

HOTEL GELLÉRT

GELLÉRT

POLLINI

1056 Bp. V., Váci u. 45. Tel.: 137

BUDAPEST

*In Vienna, an orchestra dedicated solely to Mozart's music performs in 18th-century costume.*

Vs, and fruit trees are in bloom in the countryside. Epernay, Pogny, Nancy—the towns come and go. In one small city, cathedral spires rise from a bank of fog. We run alongside a neat and tidy canal filled with placid green water and through villages that look untouched by the centuries. There are thin clouds high in the blue sky. A sudden tunnel makes my ears pop.

I have another croissant and a hot chocolate from a cart that moves along the corridor. Outside, on the canal's towpath, a man on a bicycle races a man on skates; there are houseboats and pleasure boats on the canal. In the villages every house has a TV antenna on its roof; evidently, cable hasn't arrived here yet.

The businessmen get off at Strasbourg, and we pass without incident into Germany.

Many writers have made this trip. I've just reread Graham Greene's

*Famed Viennese specialty: Sacher torte.*

*Stamboul Train* and am looking for the sort of atmosphere he wrote about: One of his characters "wondered momentarily whether something dramatic had passed close by him, something weary and hunted and the stuff of stories."

Agatha Christie set a mystery aboard the *Orient Express*. Her character Hercule Poirot describes the scene in the dining car: "It lends itself to romance, my friend. All around us are people, of all classes, of all nationalities, of all ages. For three days these people, these strangers to one another, are brought together." Several pages later: *"And now a passenger lies dead in his berth—stabbed."*

Nothing quite so dramatic troubles our passage through the German countryside. In the dining car, two Americans sit across the aisle from me. She's tired and trying to pick a fight. He offers her a bite of his

14

*Models display latest Viennese styles in a fashionable store.*

sole. She tastes it, wrinkles her nose, says, "Kind of fishy."

"Well it's a fish!" he snaps.

Full of goulash and strudel, I read and doze through the afternoon. In Stuttgart, where I paused for a day, a pale, cold sun returned. Several streets near the train station have been turned over to pedestrians and shops, all busy. Germany appears to have become a nation of shoppers. Two young Americans in baggy shorts, carrying skateboards, were unimpressed. One said, "What they need is, like, a 7-Eleven. That's what they need." I heard snatches of rap music in German, which made it sound even more obscene. A movie theater was showing *Dumm und Dümmer.*

Again riding backward, I depart Stuttgart for Vienna, passing through a park and across the Neckar River. I'm in a first-class coach, nearly empty, with nothing to worry about for seven hours except what to have for lunch and not sleeping through a change of trains at Salzburg. The conductor is a young woman, very friendly. Stations of little towns flash past too fast for me to read their names.

The inaugural trip of the *Orient Express* began on the evening of October 4, 1883,

*Laid out between 1858 and 1865, the Ringstrasse reflects the grandeur of Vienna under Emperor Franz Joseph.*

with about 40 specially invited guests and officials. It was the very first running of a transcontinental express in Europe.

Included on this run were the Paris correspondent of the *Times* of London as well as a French novelist, Edmond About. He described the coaches as "mobile homes, constructed of teak and glass, brilliantly lit by gas lamps, splendidly windowed, as well appointed and comfortable, on immediate view, as any luxury flat in Paris." In the dining car, tables were laid for four and two, and the Burgundian chef, working from a kitchen About described as "but a hand's-breadth across," served superb cuisine. The *Times* correspondent drank "wine red as rubies, white wine that gleamed as the topaz." At 50 miles an hour they thundered east, dazzled in Strasbourg and Vienna, as they had been in Paris, by stations newly lit with electricity.

A group of Gypsy musicians entertained the travelers on the platform at Szeged, then unexpectedly came aboard

Danube that this train went no farther; they had to complete the trip to Constantinople by a combination of ferry, rattling train, and ship. It was not until June 1889 that travelers could board a train in Paris and not step off until it reached Constantinople 67 hours and 35 minutes later.

*G*öppingen, Ulm, Augsburg, Endorf—the towns come and go outside my window. As is the case everywhere in the world, trackside warehouses seem to have most of their windows broken out. It's Saturday, so people are in their gardens or bicycling alongside the train. In Salzburg I have five minutes to change trains and, thanks to Austrian efficiency, make it with four to spare.

In my compartment for this leg of the trip are a middle-aged South African couple and a blowsy Austrian blonde in tight black pants and loose, floppy top; she

*One player's hand spells disaster as old friends enliven the trip to Budapest by regular train with a card game.*

the train. The musicians traveled with them for several hours, performing while the passengers danced in the dining car.

At Bucharest they had breakfast—tea and caviar sandwiches at six in the morning—at the station buffet. Passengers were shocked to learn at Giurgiu on the

immediately goes to sleep. *The Madonna of the Sleeping Cars*—the first novel to feature the *Orient Express*—had a heroine of footloose appeal: She is "an adventuress," author Maurice Dekobra wrote in his autobiography, "who travels by Pullman, seeking some hidden spot on the map of Love."

*Turkish baths at Budapest's historic Hotel Gellért feature an ornately columned swimming pool.*

*Church spires in Buda face Hungary's neo-Gothic Parliament Building across the Danube River in Pest.*

*Vibrant flower stall brightens a street in Bucharest, capital city of Romania.*

Outside the window there are miles of farms but, curiously, no farm animals. We puzzle over this. Pale Austrians sit in their yards, shirts off, trouser legs rolled up, soaking up the spring sun. The blonde wakes up and disappears for a couple of hours, somewhere in the train; when she returns, the South Africans have gone off exploring. The blonde and I are alone in the compartment. The train immediately goes into a long tunnel. The light in the compartment is dim and romantic. Suddenly I'm embarrassed and glad when we emerge from the tunnel.

At Vienna I find the window for buying my ticket to Budapest, but the agent speaks to me the phrase that strikes impotent despair into the hearts of travelers. He says, "There iss no trains in Hungary. The trains in Hungary iss on strike."

So I spent a couple of days exploring Vienna. Sunday morning I sat on a shady bench on the Opernring, reading the *International Herald Tribune* and watching runners compete in the "Vienna Spring Marathon," according to their T-shirts. Polite Austrians applauded as thousands of sweaty runners struggled past. That night I found Vienna's State Opera House—one of the world's most famous houses—and luxuriated in the lush French melodies of Massenet. The baritone was a last-minute replacement and carried the score as he sang. "At these prices," grumbled the man beside me, a doctor from Shreveport, "he should at least know his part." It was the story of Herod, Salome, and John the Baptist, which ended unhappily for just about everybody.

The train strike in Hungary turned out to be short-lived, so I was soon on my way again. The cobbled streets near the train station glistened in a soft drizzle as I boarded the train for Budapest—a run of only three and a half hours.

Getting settled, I can hear the couple in the next compartment. They're both speaking English, but in thick German accents. I wonder why they don't speak German.

I share my compartment with Louie, another South African, a young man off seeing the world. A gentle rain patters against the window as we talk. We pass officially into Hungary at the town of Hegyeshalom, and a soldier in a green uniform checks our passports.

Louie had been working as a singer and actor aboard the *Achille Lauro* a few months earlier when the ship caught fire and sank. He keeps me riveted with stories of smoke in the night, of watertight doors slamming shut, of gathering on deck, of the order to abandon ship, of bobbing in a lifeboat on the ocean as the giant ship burned nearby.

In sunshine now, the Danube sparkles as we arrive in Budapest. I took time to

*Jaunty engineer checks the platform.*

look around here, too. The streets were crowded with serious but friendly people. A taxi driver complained to me about inflation and unemployment. "Was it better under communism?" I asked. He looked shocked. "Oh, no, no! Communism was calamity!" There were new Volvos in showroom windows and bright new signs announcing "CITIBANK: 24 Hour Banking." A chilly breeze blew off the Danube, which was busy with boat traffic. Buses were crowded with standees. At night, a well-dressed, soft-spoken pimp offered "Russian girls very cheap."

In the train station, I bought my ticket

*Passengers bound for Bucharest on a regular train crowd the windows at a station in the Carpathian Mountains.*

*Ferries on the Bosporus, which divides Europe and Asia, line up near Istanbul's Süleymaniye Mosque.*

*Turkish soldier in period costume officiates at a band concert at Istanbul's Military Museum.*

for Bucharest, a 13-hour trip. I asked the agent if there would be food available on the train, and she seemed insulted. "Of course," she sniffed.

Of course, there's not—nary a morsel. No dining car, no food cart, no vending machines, nor anything to drink. It's going to be a long ride. The train is older than the trains of France and Germany—a little frayed and dusty.

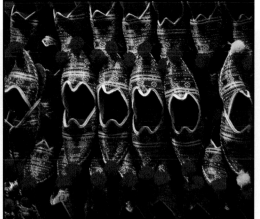
*Istanbul's bazaar offers shoes fit for a sultan's harem.*

he compartment is crowded. There is a middle-aged Romanian woman, a young Romanian couple, and a Romanian grandmother with Phillipe, her little French grandson. Phillipe has dark hair and eyes and personality to spare. He gives me a conspiratorial grin, as if we share a secret. He wiggles with happiness as he gets himself settled. His grandmother has packed for any contingency: She has three large suitcases and three overflowing shopping bags. From them emerges everything Phillipe is likely to need: food and drink, toys, books, changes of clothing, shoes, diapers, a Phillipe-size pillow and pillowcase.

Phillipe's mother, when she left him with us back in Budapest, worried about his behavior. "He's tall for his age," she said, "so people think he's older. And quieter. I hope he won't be a trouble to you."

"Maybe he'll sleep," I suggested. She looked doubtful. "Maybe...."

Phillipe soon charms everyone in the compartment. He's wearing a Dancing Mouse sweatshirt and has a stuffed lion named Leo and several books. One of them

is *Combien Ça Pèse?* He can't read, but he sits with it in his lap, his legs straight out before him, studiously turning the pages, muttering to himself. Occasionally he looks up and stretches to see out the window.

They say the American Midwest is flat, but I've never seen anything like the flatness of the Hungarian plain that we cross now—miles and miles as flat as a pool table stretching to the horizon. Square little houses squat in square little towns.

As the hours and the miles roll by and I get hungrier and thirstier, I eye Phillipe's bottomless supply of food and drink covetously and assess my chances of swiping something. Rain streaks along the window. I'm reading *To Kill a Mockingbird*. The young Romanian woman takes thick sausage sandwiches and a liter of Coke from her bag for herself and her husband. Later she helps with Phillipe, reading to him from his books.

At Chișineu-Criș we cross officially into Romania and have our passports examined. While we're stopped, I see a sign at the other side of the station, across a couple of rows of tracks: "RESTAURANT." I hurry to find the conductor. I point to the sign, then to my wristwatch, and rub my stomach. He thinks for a moment, points to *his* watch, and holds up five fingers. I scurry across the tracks and onto the platform. The restaurant is huge and empty. At the far end, near the cash register, are racks of candy bars and snacks. I gather an armful. Is that a train whistle I hear? I fling down some money and hurry back. When Phillipe sees me returning, laden with junk food, he shrieks *(Continued on page 31)*

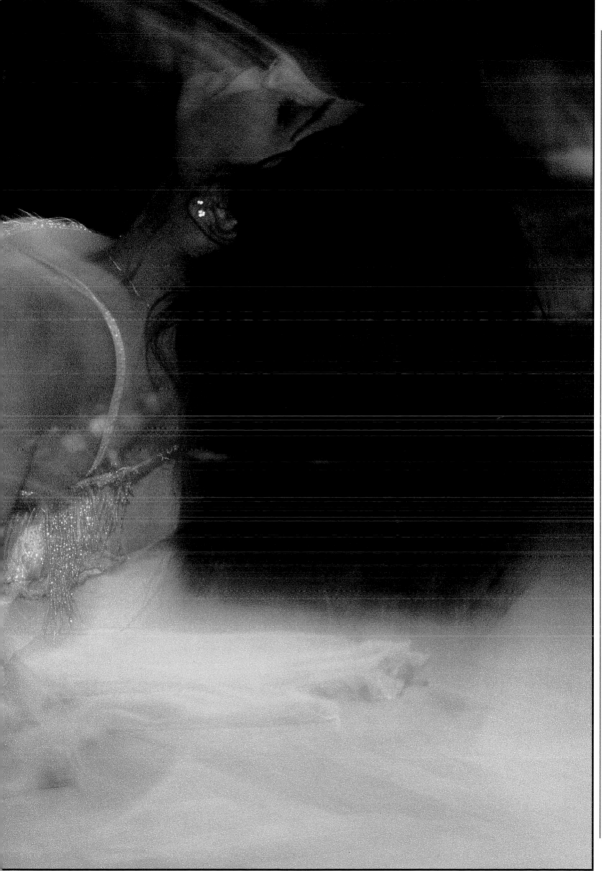

*Belly dancer at an Istanbul nightclub exemplifies the exotic lure of the Orient.*

iplomatic couriers, international spies, secret emissaries, opera singers, and foreign journalists are said to have ridden the *Orient Express* to Constantinople in the last extravagant years of the despotic Ottoman Empire before World War I. High-stakes opportunities beckoned in those dangerous, uncertain times. Foreign travelers headed for the elegant, gaslit Pera quarter in Constantinople, site of most embassies and of the luxurious Pera Palace Hotel, built in 1892 expressly to accommodate *Orient Express* passengers. Intrigue and mystery swirled around its crystal chandeliers and potted palms.

The train's aura of romance survived Constantinople's official change of name to Istanbul in 1930. Royalty, millionaires, movie stars, and writers descended on the Pera Palace Hotel between the two World Wars. Books such as Maurice Dekobra's *The Madonna of the Sleeping Cars*, Agatha Christie's *Murder on the Orient Express*, and Graham Greene's *Stamboul Train* helped establish a worldwide romantic myth about the *Orient Express*.

Though the train no longer stops in Istanbul, the Pera Palace Hotel continues to keep the myth alive.

*Greta Garbo visited the Pera Palace.*

MAGGIE STEBER

*Plaque at the Pera Palace commemorates Agatha Christie.*

# PERA PALACE HOTEL
## CONSTANTINOPLE

BOSPHORE →

← CORNE D'OR

VUE DU PERA PALACE HOTEL

*The Nostalgic-Istanbul Orient Express, a train no longer in service, steams into Istanbul's Sirkeci Station in 1984.*

*Curtained window in Venice, terminus of the revived* Orient Express, *mirrors church of Santa Maria Formosa.*

with delight. We feast through the afternoon on peanuts, pretzels, vanilla wafers, and chocolate bars.

The sun comes out and warms up the train at the same time that the register along the floor begins emitting heat. Soon it's stifling in the compartment, but it's against the rules to open the window, so we have to quickly close it whenever the conductor comes by. Phillipe gathers his toys and his pillow around him and, with a sleepy smile, stretches out on his stomach for a nap. His fingers twitch as he dreams.

I finish my book and offer it to the young Romanian woman, who speaks a little English. She's very pleased to have it, and her husband, who has seemed a little fierce, shakes my hand. Meanwhile, we pass along a quiet river and through some wooded hills. People in fields are doubled over, weeding. There are horses pulling plows and farmers carrying heavy bags on their shoulders. Phillipe wakes up, filled with energy, and is all over the compartment, but he's never a nuisance.

Phillipe and his grandmother get off at Deva, and I'm sorry to see them go. It's dark outside now, and the train is rattling and bouncing and feels as if it's going too fast for safety. There's a smell of fuel oil, and orange flares of burning natural gas appear in the darkness like beacons.

At 11 p.m., queasy from pretzels and chocolate, I stagger off the train onto the platform in Bucharest, capital of Romania, as it begins once more to rain.

In 1940 Romania's King Carol II was forced to abdicate his throne. He fled from Bucharest on the *Orient Express*, with his beautiful mistress Magda Lupescu and three carriages loaded with booty from the palace—paintings, stamp collections, books, jewelry, and Magda's suitcase full of foreign currency. He had long been accustomed to using the *Orient Express* for his own travels and also to shuffle various

*A ride on a gondola, Venice's traditional craft, provides a romantic view of the Grand Canal.*

*Piazzetta San Marco, in Venice, attracts streams of sightseers and pigeons.*

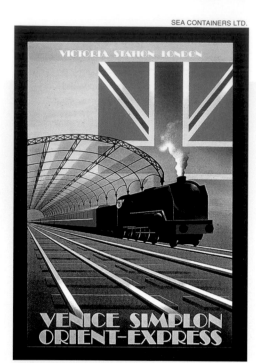

*Art deco-style poster recalls heyday of train travel.*

long, complicated announcement, which has the word Istanbul in it four times, but no one near me speaks English. I wonder if I'm on the right train.

Hundreds of people get on at Giurgiu, have their passports checked, then ride across the river to Ruse, where they get off. Who knows what's going on.

An eager young conductor named Ivan comes and sits with me between his rounds to practice his English. "The color of my

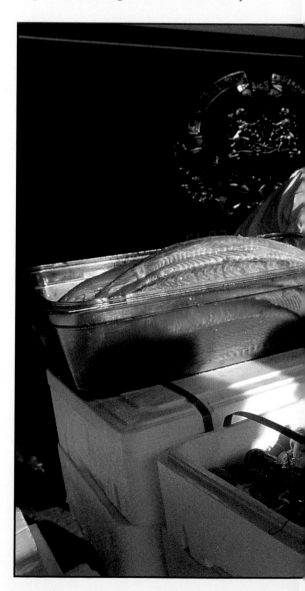

other mistresses around the continent. Partisans fired at the train in Yugoslavia, but the unseated king and his lover made it safely to Switzerland.

As I've progressed eastward across Europe, the quality of the trains has gradually fallen. The last leg of the trip is on the worst train—grungy, tattered, and smelling of toilets. I'm faced with 23 hours aboard it, from Bucharest to Istanbul, but have learned my lesson and am carrying a big bag of sandwiches, fruit, and bottled water.

Magpies are busy in the fields alongside the tracks as we roll by. Horse-drawn wagons haul loads of hay, and in the fields it's difficult to tell the old women from the scarecrows, which I guess is the whole idea. There's a two-lane concrete highway alongside the tracks being battered to rubble by big trucks.

It takes us four hours to travel the 45 miles from Bucharest to Giurgiu, where the Danube forms the Romanian-Bulgarian border. There's a long delay while passports are checked. A woman on a public-address system keeps making the same coat is blue." "The name of my son is Eactor." The train stops every ten or fifteen minutes and groans and hisses while one or two people get on or off.

In the afternoon I'm alone in my compartment and relishing the solitude when the train stops at Veliko-Tŭrnovo and a crowd of young men gets on. I'm disappointed. There goes my solitude. They come swarming onto the train, stowing baggage and getting settled.

But they turn out to be a happy surprise. They're third-year students at the Bulgarian equivalent of West Point. "We are sergeants," says one, named Milos. And, like American cadets, they are smart, polite, and well behaved. It's Friday, and they're going home for the weekend. They're fascinated to have an American on board; and though they all speak a little English, they send for Alexander, their classmate who has had the most English—

*Chef examines gourmet delights for the hundreds of meals he prepares on the Venice Simplon-Orient-Express.*

five years. "Now you can speak English, sir," says Milos.

We're going through lovely country—narrow gorges with white tumbling streams and nicely wooded hillsides—and the afternoon and evening pass quickly. When I ask the sergeants a question, they consult together on the answer, then their English expert, Alexander, who is embarrassed to be the focus of so much attention, thinks it through carefully before delivering a perfect English sentence. I ask about their studies. "At the academy," says Alexander, "as in such academies everywhere, our curriculum is a mixture of regular academic courses, such as chemistry and history, along with military subjects—tactics and command, for instance." They are slack-jawed with wonder to hear that women attend American academies along

*Alpine villages overlooking a region of lush vineyards dot the foothills en route to Verona, Italy.*

with men, and there's a lot of chortling and nudging as they contemplate such a world. One of them, with a severe crew cut, is gruff and silent and sits apart, playing a handheld video game. They are curious about illegal drugs and guns in the U.S. and shake their heads in amazement when I tell them about life in some of our large cities. They get MTV and know more about popular music than I do. They startle me

by asking, "Please, sir. Can you tell us the meaning of the word 'rednecks'?" It turns out there's a rock-and-roll group named Rednex. They like Bruce Springsteen and Elton John but not Metallica or Snoop Doggy Dogg. One is wearing a T-shirt that reads "Born Loose."

I ask if they see American movies, and they rattle off the names of studios whose movies they see: Columbia, United Artists, Paramount, TriStar. The gruff one looks up and says, "Hanna-Barbera," and everyone laughs. Someone sings the theme from *The Flintstones.*

Outside, it's so dark I think we must be in a tunnel, but suddenly there's a pinpoint of light in the distance—a lonely farm. The sergeants have taught me to say hello and good-bye in Bulgarian, so when they get off at Stara Zagora to catch other trains to their homes, I get plenty of practice.

It's nearly midnight, and I've just stretched out to try to get some sleep when we stop at another station and five men join me in my compartment, two of them drunk. The drunkest is the loudest, and he and his companion pass a vodka bottle back and forth and engage in a heated discussion. It seems to be about either politics or soccer. Through the darkened countryside we rumble. The train's whistle is a high-pitched shriek. One of Graham Greene's characters said, "I am always so afraid of travelling on a train with nothing but a lot of foreigners." One drunk gets off and the other promptly goes to sleep. I doze, sitting up, and am awakened when the last of them gets off. Alone at last, I stretch out. The last thing I see is a mouse scurrying across the floor.

At the Bulgarian-Turkish border there's a great to-do that consumes most of the night. I'm awakened first, around 1:30 a.m., by the Bulgarian conductor. We're stopped at Svilengrad, Bulgaria, and he wants to see my ticket. Half an hour later, still parked in the same station, I'm awakened by the Bulgarian police, who check my passport. The wretched train creeps a few miles forward, to Kapikule, in Turkey. At about 3 a.m. there's a great hammering on the door of my compartment by the Turkish conductor, who wants to see my ticket. Half an hour later, still in Kapikule, I'm awakened by the door sliding open with a crash and the light flicking on: Turkish passport control. This time there's some excitement. The officer looks at my passport, sucks in his breath, and motions me into the corridor. "Police!" he says.

"What?"

"Police! Police!" He thumps my passport, indicates I should bring my bag, and hustles me out the door at the end of the car. "Police," he says, pointing. The station is dark and deserted, but in the distance I see a yellow light over a door. Half asleep, shirttail flying, bag thumping against my leg, I scuttle across two rows of tracks, clamber up onto the far platform, and hurry toward the distant light.

Two policemen inside are surprised to see me, but courteous. One looks at my passport and is as troubled as the first official by what he sees. But there's a simple solution to whatever the problem is: He rummages for a rubber stamp, carefully stamps a tidy blue circle onto my visa, smiles, and sends me back to the train.

Back in my compartment I settle down to try to sleep. It's cold, so I get a sport coat from my bag to use as a blanket. I can barely believe it when, in half an hour, I'm awakened yet again by the conductor, who ushers two friends bound for Istanbul into the compartment. It means two of us will have to sleep sitting up. I'm one of the unlucky ones. I doze fitfully through the

*A stroll down carpeted corridors yields glimpses of the luxurious comfort enjoyed on board the VSOE.*

Lady's fan adds a merry flourish to the dining car of the VSOE.

remainder of the miserable night.

I am awakened by bright sunlight penetrating the thin curtain. I look out and see that, sometime in the last few hours, we've found those sunnier climes: date palms and olive trees along the tracks. Soon we're passing through Istanbul's suburbs, picking up commuters, and passing ships anchored where the Sea of Marmara narrows toward the Bosporus. Then with a hiss and a sigh we shudder to a stop in Sirkeci Station in Istanbul—ancient Byzantium, storied Constantinople, the capital of the Byzantine Empire.

Beaten and battered, grimy and sleepy, I flew the next day to Venice and, with a heartfelt sigh of relief, climbed up into the warm, capacious, all-forgiving, exquisitely opulent, and sublimely comfortable lap of luxury—today's genuine Venice Simplon-Orient-Express (VSOE). The minute I step aboard my blue-and-gold carriage, I seem to hear the welcome sound of champagne corks popping.

This most recent incarnation of the Orient Express is the work of American James B. Sherwood, millionaire hotel and sea-container magnate. In 1977 he began buying up original Pullman and wagons-lits carriages, which were scattered all over Europe. Four and a half years and 11 million pounds' worth of restoration later, he had enough of a train for an inaugural run on May 25, 1982, from London to Venice, on the former Simplon-Orient-Express

route. Now the train follows part of an old Arlberg-Orient-Express route through spectacular scenery, but misses the Simplon Tunnel. Sherwood has 17 first-class carriages, Pullmans, sleepers, and restaurant cars restored and available for service.

A white-gloved, uniformed steward named David, from the north of England, welcomes me aboard and shows me to my compartment—a single in the middle of the car, with rich upholstery and inlaid paneling. I note with alarm that it's the same compartment in which Agatha Christie's fictional murder took place. Settled in, I'm soon interrupted by the maître d'hôtel, in tails, who wonders which seating I want for lunch and dinner.

I'm in Sleeping Car 3309, which has been elegantly and painstakingly restored to its original condition. It was built in Nivelles, Belgium, in 1926. Its beautiful floral marquetry panels were created by art deco master René Prou. It operated between 1928 and 1939 on various sections of the Orient Express system, traveling as far as Munich and all the way to Istanbul via Vienna and Budapest. It was involved in several adventures. In 1929 it was part of the Simplon-Orient-Express that was marooned in a snowdrift in western Turkey for several days. Agatha Christie later borrowed the snowstorm, the marooned train, and the car for her mystery; being snowbound gave Poirot time to solve the murder. Some of the 1920s Orient Express carriages were used later in the film version.

Sleeping Car 3309 may have been part of the train that was involved in one of the Orient Express's few serious incidents: On

# Georges Nagelmackers
## *Father of the Orient Express*

*G*eorges Nagelmackers, originator of the *Orient Express*, was born in 1845 in Liège, Belgium, into a family of bankers. He grew to love the good things of life—good food, good wine, and sumptuous accommodations. It was his genius to supply them to European train travelers.

Tall, with splendid whiskers and a walking stick he was never without, he cut a fine figure in his world. He visited the United States in the late 1860s. There he met George M. Pullman, developer of comfortable railway cars with seats that could be made into bunks for overnight travel.

At about the same time, the transcontinental railway across the U.S. was nearing completion. Nagelmackers conceived the notion of a similar transcontinental train, with luxurious cars, that would travel back and forth across Europe. But Pullman's sleepers had one serious flaw, thought Nagelmackers. They were designed to convert into a sort of dormitory, with travelers lined up along both sides of a car, separated only by thin curtains. The delicate sensibilities of ladies were a concern.

*Georges Nagelmackers (1845-1905)*

Nagelmackers planned what were in effect tiny, private four-person bedrooms, with seats that converted to bunks.

A brief partnership with another American, Col. William d'Alton Mann, gave him capital enough to found his Compagnie Internationale des Wagons-Lits.

Perhaps the most difficult challenge facing Nagelmackers was negotiating rights to travel throughout Europe. It helped that Belgium's King Leopold II was an active patron of the company.

To publicize his new service, Nagelmackers hit upon the Grand Inaugural Run of the *Orient Express*, which set off from Paris for Constantinople on October 4, 1883. Like an anxious mother hen, Nagelmackers rode along, shepherding his trainload of celebrities, dignitaries, and members of the press across the continent, dealing with crises. When the dining car developed a hot axle box and had to be left behind in Munich, another was ready and waiting to replace it.

Nagelmackers saw his *Orient Express* become a resounding success, but died in 1905. The heyday of the *Orient Express* was yet to come.

COMPAGNIE INTERNATIONALE DES WAGONS-LITS (ALL)

*Inaugural run of the* Orient Express *in 1883.*

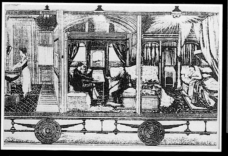

*Nagelmackers' first wagons-lits, forerunners of the* Orient Express, *held three compartments.*

September 12, 1931, a bomb went off as the engine passed over it a few miles west of Budapest. Several cars plunged into a ravine, killing more than 20 people. Josephine Baker, the famous cabaret entertainer, was aboard—she loved traveling on the *Orient Express*—and calmed the stranded passengers by singing. Later, authorities determined that the bomb was the work of a former Hungarian army officer who said he had set it "to punish atheists traveling on luxury trains.…"

Travel writer Beverley Nichols may have anticipated this incident when he wrote in the 1920s of the "so-called *train-de-luxe* which totters across Europe, falling over bridges, blundering through ravines, and waiting for a whole day at deadly-looking hamlets in strange countries."

Car 3309 was in Paris at the outset of World War II and operated in Germany from 1942 to 1945. In 1946, repatriated, it ran from Paris to Prague or Gdynia until being transferred to Portugal in 1958. It ended its service in 1971 as part of the *Sud Express* route from Irún, Spain, to Lisbon.

On time to the minute, at 10:30 a.m., we roll westward toward Verona, then north through the Italian Alps. I admire the view over a lunch served on crisp linen, with heavy silver, flowers on the table, and wine chilling in a bucket of ice. Lunch

*At Folkestone* Orient Express *passengers board British Pullman carriages for London.*

*Waiter sets an impeccable table on a Pullman diner.*

comes in courses: *Lasagne de Saumon safranée*—salmon and saffron pasta; *Mignons de Veau et Jambon de Prague sur Fondue de Radicchio*—veal medallions and sugared ham with melted Treviso chicory; *Gaufre aux Epinards*—a tiny leaf spinach waffle; sautéed new potatoes; and for dessert, *Clafoutis de Poires et Griottines au Kirsch*—a baked pear resting atop wild cherry and kirsch custard.

Well! This is more like it! D. H. Lawrence had one of his fictional characters deplore "the atmosphere of vulgar depravity" aboard the *Orient Express*, but so far I'm not troubled by it.

The chef and his staff of as many as nine work in kitchens about eight feet by ten feet. They produce five complete meals per trip for as many as 176 passengers. There's no room for baking, so the chef picks up breads along the way. In the 1,065 miles between Venice and London, if we're an average group, we will consume 600 drinks in the bar car, 90 bottles of wine, and 30 bottles of champagne. There's a staff of 40 to look after us. There are slightly more British than American passengers, and the rest are mostly French and Italian, with a few Japanese. Our average speed will be a stately 45 miles an hour.

We pass by vineyards and lush lime-

stone hills. In midafternoon, tea and pastries are served in my compartment. It's made up now for day use, with a couch with cushions and headrests. In a corner there's a washbasin with fancy soap and towels embroidered with the VSOE emblem. Fabrics and pull-down blinds for the window are copies from earlier days.

As we pass through stations and crossings, pedestrians gawk; you can see their mouths forming "*Orient Express*." There's a look of envious wonder in their eyes.

Ideally, today's *Orient Express* would make the trip all the way from London to Istanbul. To run the train economically, however, a high occupancy is necessary. Fewer passengers are interested in going all the way to Turkey. Further, there's not time to make two round-trips a week if the train goes to Istanbul.

Past Innsbruck, we hurtle westward

*A poster advertises luxury train service begun in 1926.*

*Restored first-class British Pullman parlor car includes elegant wing chairs with lace antimacassars.*

along the Inn River through magnificent countryside. As the day progresses, we'll bump against Liechtenstein, stop briefly in Zürich, pass on through Basel, and wake in the morning in France.

Writer Marghanita Laski described the pleasures of traveling in a luxurious sleeper in 1965: "Once in your sleeper after due preparation and with at least eighteen hours ahead to anticipate, total relaxation is achieved. You are safe, isolated, unburdened, in a gently rocking cradle. No one can get at you, write to you, ring you up, and around you are strangers. Usually at a moderate speed, strange, changing country slips by. Apart from the dutiful trot on the occasional platform, no effort whatsoever is called for...."

After a nap, I get into my tux for dinner. We're an elegant crowd. The lights are low, the waiters are starched and spotless, the crystal sparkles as the train rocks. Glasses, cutlery, and china are reproductions of original designs. Bud vases and glasses have heavily weighted bases, to prevent spillage as the train lurches along. Table lamps with fringed, red silk shades cast a moody light.

The ladies are in long dresses, and many of the gentlemen are in black tie. A brochure issued to passengers claims it is impossible to overdress on the Venice Simplon-*Orient-Express*. There's a young British couple across the aisle from me. She's lovely in a long, cream-colored dress; his bow tie is a riotous explosion of color. She props her chin on a fist and smiles across the table at him in a fetching manner. They appear to be in love. At her invitation, I join them for coffee after we've eaten. They're both physicians. They've left their two children at home in Sheffield and have been in Venice, celebrating their tenth wedding anniversary.

Back in my compartment after dinner, I find that it has been transformed into a bedroom. The bed is turned down, the sheets are crisp and cool, there's a fluffy wool blanket with satin edges folded up at the foot, in case I get chilly. At the head of the bed, there's a tiny hook on the wall, with a padded oval just below it: a place to hang my pocket watch in the night.

I've asked for my breakfast early, and it arrives—coffee, juice, croissants—with a discreet knock. As I finish my coffee, we pass through royal forests and along the Seine. At Paris, there's time to step off the train—in Gare de l'Est, where it all began —and compare notes with fellow passengers, some of whom are getting off here. The train's motion seemed rougher than we're accustomed to on modern trains.

Our hosts want to feed us again before Boulogne, so in midmorning, brunch is served: scrambled eggs with smoked salmon; *Langouste rôtie au Beurre de Cresson* —broiled lobster tail; potato rosettes; and a caramelized apple tartlet. Groggy from too little sleep and too much brunch, we stumble off the train at Boulogne about one in the afternoon and board a giant catamaran,

Bon voyage! *Honeymooning couple receives a cheery farewell as they depart London on the* Orient Express.

which whisks us across the English Channel to Folkestone. There we board a train made up of cream-and-brown British Pullman carriages.

The American inventor George M. Pullman began supplying the Midland Railway in England with sleeping cars in 1873. A few years later his British Pullman Palace Car Company began providing luxury cars to several English companies. Sherwood has bought all he could find, and they've been as elegantly restored as the continental cars, using original materials whenever possible. Inside, paneling of rosewood, ash, and mahogany gleams.

*I*'m in Phoenix, a first-class parlor car of 26 seats, built in 1927. It's arranged in tables for two, with comfortable wing chairs facing each other. The car's original name was Rainbow, but a fire badly damaged it in 1936; when it was rebuilt in 1952, it was given the legendary bird's name. It was the favorite carriage of Elizabeth, the Queen Mother, and has been used by Charles de Gaulle and other heads of state. It became a stationary restaurant in Lyon, France, in 1973, and was acquired by Sherwood in 1980.

We roll through the green countryside of Kent toward London. Since it's been almost three hours since we've been served a meal, a full British tea is laid before us, with crumpets, scones, teas, jams, sandwiches, and incredible, thick Devonshire cream. Stuffed like a goose and just as content, I roll into London's Victoria Station at five in the afternoon, journey ended.

I came home with many memories, a few souvenirs, and a renewed appreciation of train travel. Robert Louis Stevenson summed it up: "Herein, I think, is the chief attraction of railway travel. The speed is so easy, and the train disturbs so little the scenes through which it takes us, that our heart becomes full of the placidity and stillness of the country; and while the body is being borne forward in the flying chain of carriages, the thoughts alight, as the humour moves them...."

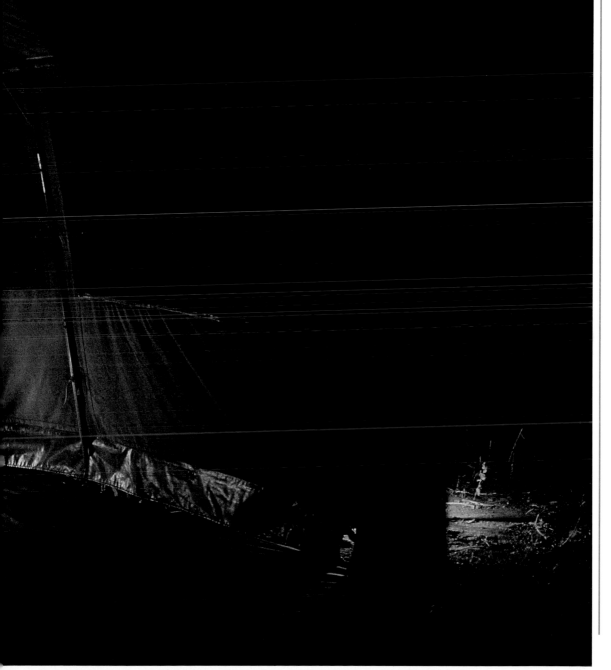

# On Safari in
# East Africa

by Patrick R. Booz
Photographs by Sarah Leen

*Evoking a bygone era of great hunters, deluxe modern safaris provide tents with amenities.*

*Ecology-minded tourism helps pay to preserve a population of lions exceeding 2,000 on Africa's Serengeti Plain.*

*I* lay in my tent rigid with fear and exhilaration. Fewer than five feet away I could hear the padding paws and deep, rapid breathing of a roving lion. All the hairs on my body stood on end, and I felt totally alive and alert, as if the African night had given me an extra sense. The lion slowly passed by. My pounding heart relaxed, allowing other sounds to fill the tent. Wildebeests grunted and croaked, sounding strangely like bull-frogs. Praying mantises whirred and struck the tent. Suddenly the darkness was cut by the weird whooplings, yips, and tremolo wails of hyenas. I peered cautiously out, but saw no creatures, only the Southern Cross low in the sky. This unfamiliar constellation, alien to northern latitudes, had become a new friend, adding to the vibrancy of all that surrounded me.

I had come to East Africa to experience firsthand the last great habitats of its amazing animals, to learn about the land, the people, and the challenges of today. Here on the Serengeti Plain my dreams of a successful safari were coming true.

The word "safari" means simply "a journey" in Kiswahili, the lingua franca of East Africa. Originating in Arabic, the borrowed word entered all the European languages as hunters and sportsmen at the end of the 1800s came in search of game and adventure. Their endeavors put a new twist on the meaning, and "safari" still summons excitement, romance, and a dash of danger. The lion's visit to my tent proved that.

My own safari began on the terrace of the Norfolk Hotel in Nairobi, where I teamed up with Sarah Leen, a first-rate photographer, energetic, ever enthusiastic. Over tea we plotted a grueling schedule while breathing in the atmosphere of this famous hotel.

The Norfolk, which opened in 1904, became the initial stop for any traveler of means to Kenya. The hotel was a spot of civilized comfort—cool rooms, clean beds, good food, stimulating company—in an otherwise dismal setting.

Only five and a half years earlier the Uganda Railway had reached Nairobi, "cold water" in the Masai language. This uninviting marsh was the last expanse of flat land before railway builders faced the engineering headaches of an escarpment climb, followed by a steep descent to the floor of the Great Rift Valley, so it was selected to be the railway's administrative center, roughly halfway between Mombasa on the Indian Ocean and the terminus at Lake Victoria in Uganda. The railway was Nairobi's raison d'être, and for nearly a century Nairobi—and especially the Norfolk Hotel—has been the point of embarkation for all safaris in Kenya.

The fledgling town was a rough-and-tumble place, a melting pot of Arab and Asian traders, European farmers, Indian laborers, Masai tribespeople, and upper-class Englishmen. Undisputed leader of the foreign settlers was Lord Delamere, a resourceful and tenacious pioneer. He worked tirelessly on his two huge estates,

*Tourist lies on groundsheet, reading safari journal.*

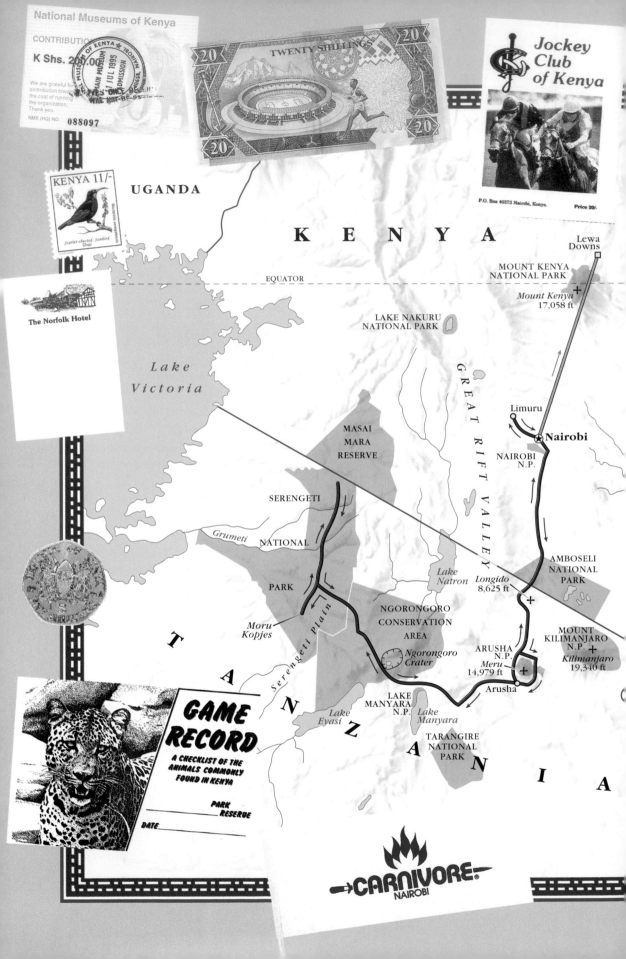

National Museums of Kenya

CONTRIBUTION
K Shs. 200.00

We are grateful for your
contribution towards
the cost of running
the organization.
Thank you.

NMK (HQ) NO.    088097

TWENTY SHILLINGS
20    20
20

Jockey
Club
of Kenya

P.O. Box 40373 Nairobi, Kenya.    Price 20/-

KENYA 11/-
Scarlet-chested Sunbird
Chalcomitra senegalensis

The Norfolk Hotel

UGANDA

K E N Y A

EQUATOR

Lewa
Downs

MOUNT KENYA
NATIONAL PARK

Mount Kenya
17,058 ft

LAKE NAKURU
NATIONAL PARK

Lake
Victoria

Limuru

Nairobi

NAIROBI
N.P.

MASAI
MARA
RESERVE

G R E A T   R I F T   V A L L E Y

SERENGETI

NATIONAL

Grumeti

PARK

Moru
Kopjes

Serengeti Plain

Lake
Natron

Longido
8,625 ft

AMBOSELI
NATIONAL
PARK

NGORONGORO
CONSERVATION
AREA

Ngorongoro
Crater

MOUNT
KILIMANJARO
N.P.

Kilimanjaro
19,340 ft

ARUSHA
N.P.
Meru
14,979 ft

Arusha

T A N Z A N I A

Lake
Eyasi

LAKE
MANYARA
N.P.

Lake
Manyara

TARANGIRE
NATIONAL
PARK

GAME
RECORD
A CHECKLIST OF THE
ANIMALS COMMONLY
FOUND IN KENYA

PARK
RESERVE

DATE

CARNIVORE
NAIROBI

KENYA

# NANYUKI

**Author's Route**

━━━ By air
━━━ By land

0                  100 mi
0                150 km

TSAVO

NATIONAL

PARK

*INDIAN*

*OCEAN*

○ Mombasa

National Museums of Kenya

CONTRIBUTION

K Shs. 50.00

9·7·95

We are grateful for your
contribution towards
the cost of running
the organization.
Thank you.
NMK (LMM)NO.

016831

*S*outhern Kenya
and northern Tanzania
lie at the heart of safari
country in East Africa,
where volcanic peaks,
soda lakes, and vast
savannas create a
diverse landscape.
The highest mountain
in Africa, snowcapped
Mount Kilimanjaro,
crowns the Great Rift
Valley region.
The traditional safari
route in Tanzania
includes Serengeti, Lake
Manyara, and Arusha
National Parks and
Ngorongoro Crater.
In addition to the
popular national parks
in Kenya, tourists can
visit Lewa Downs,
a private ranch
maintained as a
wildlife preserve, and
take a look at a tea
plantation in the lush
rolling hills of Limuru.

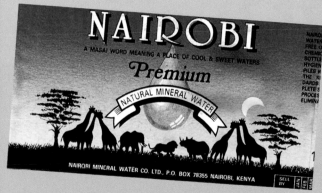

*Safari vehicles grind to a halt as an elephant emerges from roadside underbrush in Lake Manyara National Park.*

experimenting and adapting crops and animals to African conditions. He was always promoting his passion for horses.

At the heart of early Nairobi social life were the horse races. Wags commented that the first essential structures of any new colony should be the church, the jail, and the racecourse, and indeed in 1904 the first

track sprang up one mile from town. Today the track lies in the western suburbs, a vast, gently undulating oval that draws horse enthusiasts from all walks of life.

Sarah and I felt lucky to be guests of the Jockey Club of Kenya on race day, arriving at the beautiful racecourse in time to view grooms in pale turquoise coats

Italians, white Kenyans, Sikhs in turbans, even a group of eager Chinese. He turned to me with a smile and said, "We are all equal on the turf…and under the turf!" He went on to explain that horse racing is a fine equalizer and that what had once been a white domain is now a multiracial sport. "Africans are sensible. They do not bet fanatically. Some are excellent authorities on a horse's form and potential, and some are successful owners, too." The race began. Mr. Bowden excused himself,

*Common sight on safari, a lizard crawls on a tent.*

picked up his binoculars, and was lost in the excitement.

The next morning Sarah and I began our safari in earnest, heading to northern Tanzania's outstanding preserves—Arusha, Lake Manyara, and Serengeti National Parks and Ngorongoro Conservation Area. Our first guide was Francis Muigai, a Kikuyu, one of Kenya's 42 tribes. His years in the park service had led to his interest in man's interrelationship with animals. "You can call it ethnozoology, if you like; it's really about how local people are completely in tune with their environment— what they can learn from a cricket's call or the flight of a bird, how when alone in the bush, day or night, they are always completely at home." He proved to be a font of myth and lore.

The first wild animal I saw was a hartebeest, an ungainly antelope with a

parading the horses, followed by jockeys in flamboyant silks—purple and pale-blue stripes, green and red checks, pink, crimson, orange, and royal blue.

David Bowden, the club's affable managing director, invited me up to his box to watch the fifth race. I commented on the wonderful mix of people—Africans,

*By day, hippos mostly remain submerged up to their nostrils in water. They climb out at night to graze.*

long face and lumpy forehead. Francis pointed out: "That fellow, he can go without drinking for weeks or even months, so it won't help you to follow him if you are looking for water."

We passed huge earthen piles, the ubiquitous termite mounds of the African plains. Francis motioned to one and asked playfully, "You know how to catch termites for food? You need two men. One knocks two sticks together without stopping—clack, clack, clack, clack—the noise imitates the sound of falling rain. The other man pours water on the mound...and out they come, thinking it is raining. Supper!"

Some tales had the tone of Kipling's *Just So Stories*. Francis presented the story of why humans are mortal. "One day at the beginning of time, God sent the tortoise to deliver a message to humans. The message was wonderful, for it stated that human beings would never die. But the tortoise was too slow, so God became impatient and sent the hyena with a different message. The hyena arrived before the tortoise and humans learned to their dismay that they *would* die. Ever since then, death has come for every man."

I also learned that each part of the landscape—every hill, ravine, and spring—has a name. As we continued southward, a heroic mountain rose up before us, culminating in a pinnacle of sheer rock. "That is Olongido, 'The Rock Which the Masai Use to Sharpen Their Spears.'"

Time flew by as Francis's words evoked old Africa, and soon he passed us on to a new guide who would be our driver, scout, protector, and informant. This new man was a member of the Chagga tribe, inhabitants of the lower slopes of Mount Kilimanjaro. He struck me as sober,

*Snowcapped Kibo, at 19,340 feet the highest of Mount Kilimanjaro's three peaks, rises above dawn's misty veil.*

*Women in a Masai family settlement in Tanzania proudly display their prized traditional beadwork.*

responsible, unflappable. And his name was…Elvis. I knew we were in good hands. He had been the driver for Prince Charles and for Bill Gates of computer software fame, facts announced to us with no hint of bragging. More important to Elvis Barnabas Ngowi by far was his home country, "the most beautiful on earth." His eulogizing of the Kilimanjaro landscape only raised our expectations.

The second morning in Tanzania will always stay in my memory as the "Kilimanjaro Dawn." Sarah and I were up long before the sun for a rendezvous with Phil Kisamo, pilot of a single-engine Cessna. We took off at first light from the small airport at Arusha, heading east. The initial sight of the massive mountain filled me with awe; there it stood, illuminated from below by the rising sun, a sea of

"I fancied I saw the summit...with a dazzlingly white cloud. My guide called the white which I saw, merely *'Beredi,'* cold; it was perfectly clear to me, however, that it could be nothing else but snow."

Rebmann's discovery was met with ridicule by the learned men of the Royal Geographical Society of London. It was not until 1871 that an Englishman reached the snow line.

Outside the airplane's left window rose the blasted volcanic wall of Mount Meru, Tanzania's second highest peak. At nearly 15,000 feet, it was impressive and stately, though dwarfed by Kilimanjaro's 19,340-foot grandeur. Just the day before I had been close to hippopotamuses, giraffes, and Cape buffalo at the edge of Big Momella Lake. I felt akin to the African fish eagle I had seen gliding across the lake's surface, now directly below.

As the land climbed to the Kilimanjaro

clouds lapping its lower slopes. A strip of white limned the flattened summit—here were the ethereal snows of Kilimanjaro.

In the 1840s it seemed impossible to Europeans that an equatorial mountain might be snowcapped. But in May 1848 a German missionary named Johann Rebmann, already familiar with the Chagga people and their upland terrain, gazed one morning upon a majestic sight.

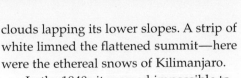
*Samburu girl in Kenya wears beads received as gifts.*

highlands, myriad specks of trees gave way to an olive-gray wasteland. I turned to catch a final glimpse of the moon; it went down as the sun came up, both orbs visible, balancing the horizons. In an instant I felt the wonder of this ancient continent and understood Ernest Hemingway's love affair with Africa and Kilimanjaro in particular. He first came here in 1933 and turned his experiences, including bush flying, into successful stories.

We swooped down toward shimmering streams; dots of brilliant water lit up the tilted, moonscape plain as we turned toward Arusha. My mind was racing with excitement. During the landing, pilot Phil pointed out brightly dressed schoolchildren in a field, some playing soccer, others marching in a straight line. The sight of people brought me back from reverie.

Driving west from Arusha toward Lake Manyara, through a semiarid landscape reminiscent of New Mexico, Elvis pulled over at a dusty gathering. "This is a tribal market, full of everything. But Sarah, you must be very careful about taking pictures. Only from far away. People here don't think kindly of photos. There might be trouble." With this warning we stepped into the hubbub, but in fact I found the market to be a friendly place. Here were the WaMeru from the slopes of Mount Meru, the WaArusha and the Masai from the south and west.

Masai men in small groups greeted one another. They carried lovingly shaped sticks of black wood with pommeled ends. Symbols of age and status, these iron-hard sticks may be used for protection, too.

Sandals cut from worn-out automobile

*Four-wheel-drive vehicles negotiate steep descents to bring tourists to the Ngorongoro Crater floor.*

tires were the ubiquitous footwear. Above the ankles men wore traditional clothing—loose fitting togas known as *shukas*, and cape-like cloths of Scotch plaid, brilliant in

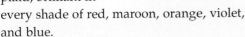

*Galloping wildebeests kick up dust on the dry savanna.*

every shade of red, maroon, orange, violet, and blue.

An elder had one ear dangling with beads and silver earrings. In the other ear he wore a glass medicine bottle—a plug in a hugely distended earlobe. With long, nimble fingers he motioned for me to approach. I had pointed to the medicine bottle, and he smiled. He looked down on me with amusement—he was so much taller—and reached for something in his voluminous cloak. His hand emerged with a dun-colored powder—snuff. Masai men love their snuff.

Others gathered around, so I had no choice but to try it. As soon as it entered my nostrils, a sharp sting filled my head; we all laughed as my eyes grew wide and watery at this new sensation.

The market offered every kind of food and useful commodity imaginable: purple sugarcane, mounds of beans, rice, maize, shiny red peppers, mountains of onions, bananas by the thousands, heaps of firewood, boxes of glass beads, soap, pots, buckets, knives, kerosene. Churning up dust were innumerable battered vehicles—pickups, vans, Jeeps. One Land Cruiser was crammed with 18 people, all of them shouting and gesticulating and buying goods from women with baskets and bundles balanced on their heads.

In front of this scene sauntered two Masai lads, young warriors known as *moran*, who were proud and cocky in all their finery. They carried long, sharp spears that towered above their heads. Their hair was worn long, beaded, and dyed russet red like rusted chain mail. One of the warriors wore a headband that culminated in a triangular silver pendant on his forehead.

Braying, jabber, laughter, and dust flew from every direction. The air was redolent with fried tidbits of meat and vegetables. Pack donkeys stood patiently in the shade of a giant fig tree, tethered two deep. As we departed, a woman drifted by like a yellow butterfly in the brilliant sunshine. She wore lemon- and ochre-colored clothing and balanced a frond basket piled high with golden maize on her head.

We pressed on over bad roads to Lake Manyara, one of Tanzania's smallest national parks, but a gem. The lake and protected lands lie beneath the Rift Escarpment, an eastern spur of the Great Rift Valley, the massive fault that runs from Mozambique to the Red Sea. Just beyond the entrance gate stands a dense forest—lush, dark home to lithe blue monkeys and a troop of wary baboons. They screeched and fled as we passed to drier, more open acacia woodland, where immediately we came upon a herd of elephants.

One young male elephant stood at the edge of a muddy water hole. First he splashed his belly, using his trunk as a hose, seeming to grin with pleasure at the cooling effect. He showered water over his back and forehead, then gently put his legs into the water, slowly rising with glistening knees. Finally, the versatile trunk created a

*Morning mist swirls among euphorbia trees on the Ngorongoro Crater wall.*

miniature dust storm all around him. In a few efficient minutes the elephant cooled off and protected his skin from the hot sun and from irritating insects.

On the escarpment Sarah spotted a cluster of baobab trees. We investigated these huge, gray, smooth-barked peculiarities, among the oldest living trees on earth. Carbon dating has revealed some to be 3,000 years old;

*Young Masai girl blinks at dawn's first light.*

Portuguese cannon balls from the 1500s have been found embedded in living baobabs. The tree, emblematic of the African landscape, appears inverted, as if the roots are growing into the sky; local legend accounts for this by saying that God, in a rage, uprooted the baobab and turned it upside down forever. Its massive trunk stores water, and an individual tree can grow more than 80 feet tall. In times of drought, elephants gouge out a baobab trunk for water, sometimes causing the tree to collapse.

Below us spread the expanse of Lake Manyara. Rich light from the setting sun ignited the pink of thousands of flamingos feeding in the shallow waters. The birds extended for miles in broken lines; again and again flocks would rise up from the lake's surface like a pink mist, utterly mesmerizing as the clouds of color drifted and settled anew.

*"Ex Africa semper aliquid novi*—Always something new out of Africa." These words quoted by Roman scholar Pliny the Elder in the first century A.D. spoke to me directly and never so strongly as when facing the Ngorongoro Crater.

Thirty-eight years ago Bernhard and Michael Grzimek, a father-and-son team of zoologists from Germany, came to this region to undertake the first thorough survey of the land and its animals. As scientists they avoided hyperbole, but Ngorongoro was something different. "It is impossible to give a fair description of the size and beauty of the crater, for there is nothing with which one can compare it. It is one of the Wonders of the World." I concurred as we descended onto the vast crater floor, a plain of yellow grass 2,000 feet below steep walls. Entering the Ngorongoro Crater was like stepping into the dawn of the world. The first dizzying sights were zebras and wildebeests in profusion, then a sprinkling of Thomson's gazelles, alert and graceful in their movements, unmistakable with a black racing stripe on each side.

The crater is a utopia with niches for a multitude of living things, from the smallest rodents to mighty quadrupeds. Elvis told us to keep our eyes on a spot in the distance. At first we saw nothing, then Sarah and I watched intently as a black rhinoceros emerged from high grass, trailed by her calf, trotting hard to keep up.

Fewer than 20 black rhinos exist here, and only two calves. All of them are protected day and night by armed rangers. This is no extravagance, I realized, when hearing Elvis's statistics on the black rhino: In 1970 Africa had 70,000; today the

*Hungry members of a pride intently watch lionesses heading off to hunt in the Masai Mara Reserve.*

*Tents with washbasins, folding chairs, and tables exemplify the comforts of a Serengeti safari camp.*

number has plummeted to around 2,500.

On safari I usually stood in our vehicle, feet braced, arms and head sticking out of the pop-top roof, wind blowing freely in my face. Driving along a rise we came upon a pride of lions, three mothers and at least seven cubs, the youngsters gamboling and suckling in a jumbled mass.

At day's end, Ngorongoro's Lerai Forest seems luminous. The yellow-barked acacia trees provide a favorite haunt for elephants. Around 70 bulls come and go here—magnificent, virile creatures.

I emerged from a daylong visit in the crater with a peculiar elation and spiritual refreshment. The grasses gave off a spiced, aromatic fragrance. The swiftness of the equatorial sunset startled me; the last fading light ebbed away and became true darkness in just 15 minutes.

Inside Serengeti National Park I soon noticed the unmistakable ostrich, a strutting, 300-pound bundle of feathers and skin, the world's largest living bird.

Though never a keen birder, I was completely seduced by Africa's dazzling avifauna. Even my casual sightings produced a list of 10 or 15 new species every day. By the end of the second week I had seen more than 150 types of birds, some, such as sunbirds and bee-eaters, sublime in their brilliance and delicacy, others wonderful in their personalities.

My favorite was the secretary bird, *Sagittarius serpentarius*. This long-legged predator stalks the savanna, searching for snakes, small rodents, and large insects. It strides with long, black "plus fours," and its crown feathers resemble quills tucked behind the ears of clerks.

The lilac-breasted roller is perhaps Africa's loveliest bird. Once sighted, this lilac, sky-blue, and tawny-brown marvel stole a piece of my heart, and I longed to see it again and again. It is called a "roller" because, when courting, the birds put on an acrobatic spectacle, tumbling and rolling through the air.

Camp life on the Serengeti provided a taste of bygone days in East Africa. Sarah and I were fortunate—even spoiled—to have a "full camp," efficiently run by a head bearer, assistant, cook, and camp manager. Our base was a place called Moru Kopjes, an island of upthrust rocks in the otherwise flat, grassy plain.

*Side mirror helps Elvis the guide shave.*

Before dawn, tea and biscuits arrived silently. The first morning I sat up blearily and smiled to thank Geoffrey Philip Orio, the assistant, then surveyed my little tent with satisfaction.

The bed was a proper one, sturdy and firm. Next to it stood a writing table covered with a cheerful patterned cloth and propped at its end was a wood-framed mirror. Light for the interior of the tent came from an oil lamp, and gleaming just outside was a hurricane lamp "to keep the lions and beasties away." Hot water never failed for early shaving or evening showers, which were conducted alfresco, staring up at the twinkling stars.

We dined opulently in a mess tent. Breakfast seemed to go on forever—juice, cereal, toast, oatmeal, soft-boiled eggs, pancakes, and sausages. Lunch was invariably too large; and dinner was drawn out into a four- or five-course affair, with wine, china, candles, and fine cutlery.

The greatest joys of camp life, though,

*Cook John Wilson Maturo prepares green beans for the evening meal in the mess tent.*

had nothing to do with luxury. Peace and ease were the spoils, simply having the time to sit, read, think, and pay close attention to splendid starlings, insect sounds, impalas in the distance, the blue-and-red agama lizard on a nearby rock, a spider weaving its web.

One afternoon as I sipped a cup of tea, savoring the hot liquid, my thoughts drifted to a friend I had made earlier—Evelyn Mitchell, a stalwart of the tea country around Limuru, northwest of Nairobi. Born in 1909, she is said to be the oldest surviving European born in Kenya and still living there.

Her father, A. B. McDonell, an indomitable Scotsman, became the first person to grow and make tea in Kenya. He discovered that tea could do well at 7,200 feet, where coffee would fail, and began growing it in 1918 in these lush hills. The early decades were ones of experimentation, but he remained optimistic.

"Our first house was built on this farm, 350 acres bought from the British government in 1910 for two rupees an acre. Gradually it was destroyed by white ants. What to do? Well, look around you." With a sweep of her arm she took in the fine stone house built in 1930 and perfect garden of her magnificent estate. "Yes, this is what we did to defeat the little brutes."

She explained everything about tea, from planting and growing to plucking and processing. She paused, smiling down at her Jack Russell terrier, "That's Tetley; he knows all about tea." Upon leaving she called out to us Americans, "Now cut out this coffee lark and drink more tea!"

Suddenly I was brought back to the present moment in the Serengeti by hoots,

*Burchell's zebras pass single file through high grass. Each one's pattern of stripes marks it as a distinct individual.*

*Hot-air balloonists float silently above the Serengeti Plain for unparalleled views of wildlife.*

*Spotted coat provides camouflage for a cheetah yawning in the midday heat on the Serengeti.*

*Aproned pluckers gather at day's end to weigh tea leaves. A top worker can pluck 60 to 100 pounds a day.*

shouts, and the hilarious sight of our cook chasing after a scampering baboon. The thief had stolen a box of cornflakes, never to be seen again.

Returning to camp one day, Elvis veered onto a sidetrack, having spotted something we had not seen. An abrupt halt brought us to two lions gorging themselves. They lay on their stomachs, faces smeared with blood up to the ears. The victim was a wildebeest. We were close enough to hear the tearing of sinews and crunching of bones. The only pest for the lions was a bold hooded vulture that crept up to the carcass to steal a bite. The lions roared at the scavenger; it retreated for a moment, only to sneak up again for another mouthful.

We watched as the lions filled up on meat—enough to last them for three or four days. On the Serengeti Plain the abundance of life means much death as well. Nature's endless cycle assures the obliteration of individuals but the continuation of species.

Sarah and I chose to end our Serengeti visit with a hot-air balloon flight. At dawn a cluster of travelers gathered at the takeoff site to meet the two pilots, Alain Sarrasin and Bruno Dupuis. These amiable Frenchmen assured us of the balloons' safety—"Just follow zee instructions we geeve, sit and hold zee straps on landing"—and then we were off, eight people in each wicker basket. My companions were from London, travel agents here to learn about Africa. This cheerful lot, chattering like mad on the ground—"This'll sure beat being stuck in traffic on the Fulham Road"—were, like myself, utterly silenced by the extraordinary beauty of what lay below us.

Upon liftoff the morning breeze caught our balloon, colored green-and-yellow specifically to match the Serengeti landscape, and sent us drifting at five miles an hour. As we rose, the balloon cast a great elliptical shadow across the savanna. Giraffes loped like miniature stick animals 500 feet below us.

As the hot air cooled, we descended slowly to drift along the Grumeti River, home to some of the world's largest crocodiles. I looked hard with my binoculars for the huge reptiles—referred to in some places as "flat dogs"—but saw only bobbing gray lumps partially submerged. Suddenly, a hippo thrust up its head and gaped as I stared directly into its enormous pink maw.

The balloon climbed higher and higher, up to 1,500 feet, with clear views in all directions. Far below I could see a small herd of zebras—"tiger-horses"—resting their heads on each other's backs. During the final descent a startled genet sprang from the scrub to get out of the way.

We came down with a gentle bump and dragged a short way, sending up a cloud of dust. Land Cruisers had raced to bring us a special treat, and our pilots scrambled to do the honors. There, out on the open plain at 7:30 in the morning, the delicious air was filled with the sound of popping champagne corks. Our little party, animated and full of laughter, grew giddier by the moment. For a brief hour and a half the silent flight had given us new eyes with which to see the animals and the land.

Alain encouraged us to move on, so we piled into the waiting vehicles for the short trip to our breakfast site. And what a welcome! There under a flat-topped acacia tree stretched a long table, set with tablecloth, silver, and glasses.

Next to the road a striking figure dressed in a turban and robes trimmed with gold brocade poured cool water from a pewter ewer for us to wash our hands. The service was impeccable as we ate our fill under the brightening sky.

After a daylong drive to the Kenyan-

*Rolling tea fields in the Limuru region near Nairobi help make Kenya one of the world's major tea exporters.*

# K a r e n   B l i x e n :

*I*n 1914 a talented, vivacious 28-year-old arrived at the port of Mombasa, Kenya, and married her fiancé, Bror Blixen, the next day. The two proceeded inland to Nairobi to take up life as coffee farmers, thus beginning a tale of adventure that remains at the heart of East African lore and romance.

Karen Blixen, known to the world by her nom de plume, Isak Dinesen, grew up by the sea in Denmark, in a large, wealthy family. An early interest in art led her to Copenhagen's Royal Academy of Fine Arts. After leaving the academy, she suffered from unrequited love for a young Swedish baron. Seeking freedom, but also desiring a titled name, she married Bror, the baron's twin brother, and commenced her life in Kenya far from Europe's fetters.

"I had a farm in Africa, at the foot of the Ngong Hills," begins her renowned work *Out of Africa,* published in 1937. A highly popular film of the same name came out in 1985. The Blixen farm was one of the largest plantations in Kenya— 6,000 acres— and Karen cared for the land passionately. It took years for her to

*Karen Blixen, age 32, on safari in 1918.*

realize that the plantation was unsuited to growing coffee successfully. "She loved that damn coffee, she wouldn't understand that it was hopeless, even if her friends tried to tell her so," recounted one of her best friends.

After less than a year of marriage Karen contracted syphilis from Bror, a robust, devil-may-care man who ate, drank, rode, hunted, and philandered with great gusto. She went to Denmark for treatment, which achieved some success, though the rest of her life was plagued by ill health and bouts of depression. She and Bror separated in 1921 and were finally divorced in 1925.

In spite of setbacks, Karen Blixen gathered around her a fascinating household of servants, visitors, and friends. Loyal Farah, the Somali majordomo; Kamante, the eccentric cook; and crusty Old Knudsen, the blind Dane, all jump to life in the pages of *Out of Africa.* Unforgettable, too, were the *ngomas,* great dance festivals held on her grounds with up to 2,000 flamboyant Kikuyu tribespeople. Life offered an ever changing spectrum of nature, animals, and personalities.

Influential above all in her development as a person and a writer

*Happiest when "in the bush," Karen Blixen poses outside her field tent in 1914.*

# Compelling Storyteller
## Isak Dinesen

was Denys Finch Hatton, son of an earl, Oxford educated, supremely gifted physically, one of Africa's famous white hunters. He and another great friend, Berkeley Cole, a refined, fatalistic man, awakened in her a vision of life's grandeur.

Karen was devoted to Finch Hatton, for he fulfilled all her ideals. He encouraged her to write, and the life they shared—hunting lions on safari, quoting poetry, flying in his Gypsy Moth over the highlands and plains—helped bring out her inherent gifts of storytelling.

The year 1931 brought tragedy. Denys Finch Hatton died in an airplane crash. The farm had been sold, and Karen returned to

Denmark, never again to set foot in Africa. The return to the house of her birth, however, gave her time to write and to apply her mind to the world of creativity that Finch Hatton had opened.

Karen Blixen is remembered for her distinctive, timeless stories, told in evocative prose. *Seven Gothic Tales*, published in 1934, was an immediate success. Over the years her literary fame grew, with other works such as *Winter's Tales*, *Last Tales*, and *Babette's Feast*. She died in 1962 and was buried on the family grounds in a simple grave under a huge beech tree, with a handful of African soil mixed with the earth of her native Denmark.

*A Nairobi suburb, named Karen in her honor, grew up around Blixen's home, now maintained as a museum.*

Tanzanian border we said our last good-byes to loyal Elvis. As we headed north, he headed home for some well-earned rest in the shadow of his beloved Mount Kilimanjaro.

As the final leg of our safari, Sarah and I visited a private ranch just north of the Equator. For three generations the Craig family has lived at Lewa Downs, a kind of mini-Serengeti of 40,000 rolling acres within sight of Mount Kenya's twin spires. Will Craig, tall, thoughtful, soft-spoken, picked us up in a tiny airplane and flew us to a dirt landing strip on his land. Aardvarks had been digging holes there so he had to touch down carefully.

Lewa Downs is the site of a bold effort to combine ranching, tourism, and conservation. Our host explained the plan. "Seventy percent of all Kenya's wildlife survives on land outside the parks and preserves. No amount of international good-will is going to save our game unless we Kenyans live sensibly alongside the wildlife. And here we have a unique chance. In time, joining with adjacent farms, we hope to create the world's largest private conservation area."

Lewa Downs offers an exciting activity for visitors. I was up at dawn with the bleating cries of gregarious go-away birds, ready for a horseback ride in the bush. My steed knew the way; and before I was fully awake, I found myself in the midst of a herd of giraffes.

They did not fear the horse's approach, carrying on with their browsing, gazing down at me with large bedroom eyes. I could examine the Grevy's zebra, nature's work of op art, with many more tightly arranged stripes than the Burchell's zebra. I valued the freedom of this morning,

something unobtainable in a motor vehicle.

I stopped for tea with Tony Dyer, former head of the East African Professional Hunters Association, to learn of the fate of traditional safaris. A neighbor of the Craigs, he is a white hunter emeritus from the old days. The term "white hunter" did not arise from bombast, but rather is thought to have stemmed from a simple distinction attributed to Lord Delamere. He

*Spotlight captures a lone black rhinoceros at Lewa Downs, where a conservation project protects 41 rhinos.*

had two armed men to hunt predators on his land, one an Abyssinian, the other a Scotsman. To keep the two straight he simply called the latter the "white hunter."

Rose Dyer, Tony's friendly, matter-of-fact wife, showed me into the living room, a warm, welcoming place with comfortable chairs, old books, family photographs, and a fireplace. This was headquarters for their farm, Ngare Ndare, "river of sheep."

In came Tony, trim, erect, calm. His eyes, cheerful and serious at the same time, reflected both his optimism and the grave changes he has experienced through a lifetime in East Africa. He began his tale:

"In the old days, we hunters dealt with a splendid elite of people. Our clients represented the finest of manhood. As the leader, I was responsible for everything; I was a kind of captain. But the classic safari

*Former hunter Tony Dyer with his dog Buckle.* `

could only exist for a short time. It had to die, and it will never come again. A bit like the clipper ships. They had their time and glory, but events overtook them. I just feel lucky to have been a captain along the way," Tony related.

I wondered about his glory days. Tony turned his mind to the past. "During my first 24 months as a hunter I spent 15 of them in the bush. Safaris averaged five months apiece. Who has that kind of time now? Back then we had plenty of time," he reflected with satisfaction.

And the animals. He pondered for a moment. "Buffalo is the finest sporting animal on earth. All its senses are highly developed—ears, eyes, nose. It takes a lot of killing. The largest buffalo ever taken had 58-inch horns at the widest point. Imagine, that's nearly five feet. But if wounded he can finish you off as you try to finish him off." At this Tony Dyer chuckled and said nonchalantly, "I've had a buffalo horn right through my thigh."

The automobile, the airplane, and population growth changed safaris forever. But internal rot played its part as well. Tony explained, "At the very basis of hunting is an

*Giraffes at Lewa Downs let visitors on horseback photograph them up close.*

ethical relationship to the animals. This means knowing what is fair, and above all respecting the creatures and their habitats. The breakdown in ethical standards virtually ruined the old-style safari. Hunting too much, doing anything for money. And of course the ecological deterioration."

Tony Dyer is very conscious of the mortality of this country. "Forty years ago I could walk for three days and never see another human. Just me and the animals. Now there are 5,000 people here, and this delicate land can't support such numbers."

This dire comment brought to mind an interview with Anna Merz, another neighbor and a world authority on rhinos. "Fifty years ago, Africa was a great wilderness with a few patches of cultivation. Now it is mostly cultivation with a few patches of wilderness."

*Lewa Downs guests swap tales around a blazing campfire at safari's end.*

It is this very deterioration that Anna Merz, the Craigs, and the Dyers are trying to halt. Sarah and I experienced the fruits of their efforts during a thrilling night drive. A spotlight cutting through the dark at first lit up only isolated patches of scrub and trees. Then, miraculously, the night began to fill with eyes. There! The disembodied orange-red eyes of the bush babies moved erratically in the dark like pairs of luminous yo-yos. Giraffes created a strange sight in the night, their long necks and humorous-looking heads rising up as if trying to nibble the moon.

We followed a pair of eyes that were not immediately identifiable. The Jeep went slowly bouncing through the grass, closer, closer, toward the waiting eyes. Hyenas skulked away with their ever guilty look. Our driver, Daniel, whispered "animal downtown," a whimsical Africanism for an area where creatures cluster together for water or food.

Wandering in this tight zone we saw bush babies, waterbucks, hyenas, a civet, giraffes, Thomson's gazelles, and a herd of impalas race off in a brown blur.

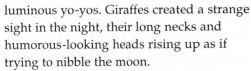

And now before us was a leopard in all its nobility. This great cat, staring back in complete composure, brought to mind Tony Dyer's observation. "The leopard must be considered the finest of the cats. In comparison a cheetah is a pathetic thing, and lions are crude. Never underestimate it. I know of an incident where five armed men went after a wounded leopard. In the time it takes me to say these words—about five seconds—the mighty cat charged like lightning from its hiding place and mauled every one of them, biting and tearing as it went. Then the leopard disappeared into the bush." I looked upon this spotted specter in the night with the utmost respect.

Respect, admiration, awe. These are the words that stay with me when I recall my weeks in Africa. The lessons and wisdom of the land, the intimate details and overwhelming grandeur, remain unforgettable in my memory as I wait to return for another journey of discovery. I hope the animals will still be waiting too.

# A Royal Train Through
# Rajasthan

by Cynthia Russ Ramsay
Photographs by Sarah Leen

*Celebration of Republic Day on January 26 in New Delhi illuminates Rashtrapati Bhawan, India's White House.*

*Antique steam locomotive pulls the* Palace on Wheels *into Delhi as a grand finale for its eight-day excursion.*

he sacred fire will soon be lit, for the procession has arrived. "And where are the garlands?" shouts Krishna Chandra Pal, maharaja of Karauli, as he hurries to greet the bridegroom's party. The music of drums, flutes, and horns stops on a long, concluding note as the groom, Ajit Singhji, splendid in his brocaded coat and plumed turban, alights from his elephant. He strikes the gate with an upraised sword, symbolizing his promise to defend his bride, a descendant of warrior-caste Rajputs who ruled the kingdom of Karauli for almost ten centuries; she is also someone the bridegroom barely knows.

"Our families thought we were a suitable match," says Shruti Kumari, a dainty, veiled figure in red, the traditional, auspicious color for a Hindu bride.

"Astrologers were consulted. Our horoscopes tallied well, so a meeting was arranged. We were given a few days to make this decision," she tells me after she has spoken her vows and taken the ritual seven steps round the fire with her bridegroom that seal the marriage.

The pageantry of a royal wedding was an appropriate prelude to a train tour of Rajasthan, fabled land of the Rajputs—"sons of kings." The modern state of Rajasthan is made up of 22 former kingdoms known collectively as Rajputana, whose rulers lived in extravagant splendor until their domains were incorporated into the newly independent Republic of India in 1947. The glamorous women

around me in the tent, draped in gorgeous, gold-trimmed silks and adorned with jewels, are descendants of women who were raised in palaces guarded by eunuchs and inhabited by multitudes of maidservants. In another tent are the men, wearing bright turbans, long coats known as *sherwanis*, and long, curved swords. These mustachioed aristocrats are heirs to a knightly tradition of chivalry and valor, forged when Rajput clans began carving out kingdoms for themselves around the seventh century A.D.

During its weeklong circuit of Rajasthan, the *Palace on Wheels* tourist train stopped at the cities of Jaipur, Chittorgarh, Udaipur, Jaisalmer, Jodhpur, and Bikaner, the former capitals of Rajasthan's largest princely states. In their long history these kingdoms were ruled by heroic conquerors, scholars, astronomers, and patrons of the arts. Some who came to the throne were ostentatious pleasure seekers. Others built irrigation systems, railways, and schools.

They traveled in grand style, with courtiers, retainers, chefs, and bodyguards. To attend receptions of the British viceroy in New Delhi or on state visits to each other, these potentates went by rail in their own custom-built carriages, emblazoned with their coats of arms.

Some of these royal carriages were assembled to start the unique *Palace on Wheels* tourist train, a bright idea of Indian Railways, which was executed by the Rajasthan Tourism Development Corporation. The train set out on its inaugural run from Delhi on January 26, 1982.

*Railway insignia adorns a* Palace *car.*

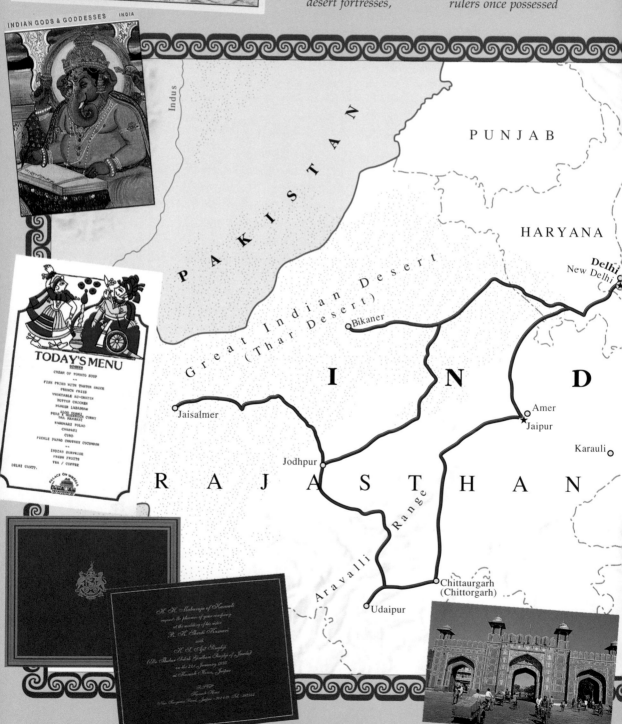

*T*hrough Rajasthan, the fabled land of maharajas, the Palace on Wheels *train* takes tourists on a weeklong journey to desert fortresses, hilltop citadels, and extravagant palaces. Formed from the merger of 22 princely states, Rajasthan sprawls across more than 130,000 square miles of northwest India. The rulers once possessed

INDIAN GODS & GODDESSES   INDIA

**TODAY'S MENU**

DINNER

CREAM OF TOMATO SOUP

FISH FRIED WITH TARTER SAUCE
FRENCH FRIES
VEGETABLE AU-GRATIN
BUTTER CHICKEN
PANEER LABABDAR
ALOO JHANGI
PEAS MUSHROOM CURRY
DAL MAKHANI
KASHMARI PULAO
CHAPATI
CURD
PICKLE PAPAD CHUTNEY CUCUMBER

INDIAN SURPRISE
FRESH FRUITS
TEA / COFFEE

DELHI CANTT.

PALACE ON WHEELS

Indus

P A K I S T A N

PUNJAB

HARYANA

**Delhi**
New Delhi

Great Indian Desert
(Thar Desert)

○ Bikaner

I     N     D

Jaisalmer ○

○ Amer
Jaipur ★

Karauli ○

Jodhpur ○

R A J A S T H A N

Aravalli Range

Chittaurgarh
(Chittorgarh) ○

Udaipur ○

*private railways and traveled in elegant coaches to go on tiger shoots, to imperial receptions in New Delhi, and, in summer, to the hills.*

CHINA

Area Enlarged

New Delhi

I N D I A

Bombay

Calcutta

NEPAL

U T T A R
P R A D E S H

I          A

Agra

Ganga (Ganges)

| 0 | 100 mi |
| 0 | 150 km |

Author's Train Route

M A D H Y A
P R A D E S H

PALACE ON WHEELS

A Rendezvous of

BREAKFAST
AND
SERVICE CARD

Shall we blow the trumpet to announce the call of the new day.
( ) Yes  ( ) No. at ( ) A.M.
How would you like to be welcomed ?
over (...... Tea with/without Milk/with Lemon ( ) Coffee with /
without Milk
I want to have my Breakfast between
( ) 7.00 - 7.30 A.M. ( ) 7.30 - 8.00 A.M.
At dream break greet-the-queen with fruit juices (small)
( ) Mango  ( ) Orange  ( ) Pine Apple  ( ) Tomato
And Multiple your Calories with
( ) Omelette  ( ) Fried  ( ) Scrambled  ( ) Poached
( ) Boiled  ( ) Mins
Or be a vegetarian for a while with
( ) Peari Bhaji  ( ) Stuffed Paratha  ( ) Vegetable Cutlets
But achieve the waistline of the Rajasthani Billionaire, with ( ) Toast
(Served with butter and fruit preserves)
And vibrate off with ( ) Tea ( ) Coffee

Name_____ Signature_____
Saloon/Coach No _____ Coupe _____
Berth _____ Upper/Lower _____
Date _____ Pax _____

PALACE ON WHEELS

Rajasthan

*Guided by a turbaned mahout, a gaily painted elephant lifts its trunk in salute to* Palace *passengers in Jaipur.*

Those royal coaches no longer exist. The interiors, which were deteriorating, were gutted, and their crystal chandeliers, mahogany bureaus, chairs upholstered in velvet, silver door handles, and porcelain soap dishes disappeared. The original carriages were refitted and used for a while, but they too were soon replaced.

The *Palace on Wheels* train that photographer Sarah Leen and I boarded at 7 p.m. in the Delhi Cantonment Railway Station was not opulent, but it was comfortable enough. Each of the 13 coach cars had four two-berth compartments with wooden paneling on the walls, brocaded bedspreads, curtains on the windows, brass lamps, and a vanity table. Each coach also had two bathrooms, with plenty of hot water for showers, and a small lounge. There was nothing sumptuous—

*Silver urn once hauled holy water for a Jaipur maharaja.*

except the service provided by two cabin attendants, impeccably turned out in crimson turbans and coats, tightly buttoned from neck to waist. Jagdish Prasad Jat— J. P.—and Prem Singh greeted us with broad smiles and palms pressed together at the forehead in the traditional *namaskar.*

"Welcome, memsahibs."

The attendants helped Sarah and me unpack and urged us to use the buzzers to call for tea, soda, fruit, or laundry service. Then, resting on plump pillows and ironed sheets, we slept as the train clattered through the night toward Jaipur.

I awakened as the sky was turning from pearl gray to pink, giving shape to the hills of the Aravalli Range, which loomed like low storm clouds above the plains. Along the track, the gnarled acacia trees

*Decked in finery, a Rajasthani woman welcomes tourists to Jaipur with marigold garlands.*

*High above the town and fortified palace of Amer, Jaigarh Fort once guarded access to Jaipur.*

were green, but in January the fields were bare. Smoke from cow-dung fires drifted in a veil above the villages. Women in full skirts that swirled above heavy silver anklets strode with brass water pots on their heads, signaling day had begun in rural Rajasthan. For me it began with bed tea, served when J. P. came to take our breakfast order, which we ate cozily in our compartment.

When the train pulled into the Jaipur station, we saw streams of intent commuters on the way to work, wearing jackets or shawls against the morning cold. They carried their lunches in "tiffin-carriers," stacked pans fitted together in a metal brace. Some travelers were villagers on a real milk run, identified by the wide-lipped milk cans carried on their heads.

At the station exit, we were met by a welcoming committee, which included two caparisoned elephants, a drummer, and a flutist. While the music played and the elephants yawned, two brightly clad women garlanded each of the more than 120 *Palace* passengers. A number of them were from the United States and Great Britain, and a good many were Indians living abroad and visiting India—some for the first time.

Buses with local guides were waiting to transport us for a daylong tour of Jaipur, once the center of a princely state roughly 15,500 square miles in area and now capital and busy commercial center of Rajasthan.

A pink, crenellated wall with seven gates encloses the old city, founded in 1727 when Maharaja Sawai Jai Singh II moved down to the plain from Amer, a hilltop stronghold about seven miles to the north. With a population of nearly two million, the metropolis has outgrown the wall, but the old quarter retains its distinct identity. Its graceful architecture of scalloped arches,

*Hooded cobra dances for Jaipur snake charmers as it sways to keep their hands in line for a strike.*

*Stone latticework of Jaipur's Palace of Winds concealed the royal women as they observed the passing scene.*

dainty pillared cupolas, and curved eaves with their eccentric droop, all in pink terracotta, make the city look like a fanciful illustration in a book of fairy tales.

Though the main avenues were wide and straight, we moved through the "pink city" en route to Amer in a crawl of cars, overloaded trucks, jam-packed buses, motor scooters, scooter rickshas, motorbikes, bicycles, cycle rickshas, camel carts, horse-drawn carts, handcarts, and darting pedestrians. Ambling in the middle of all this were the itinerant sacred cows.

Perched on a rocky spur, Amer is the quintessential medieval Rajput fortress-palace, utterly extravagant in spirit with its turrets, parapets, cupolas, and bastioned ramparts—an Indian rendition of Camelot.

Elephants and their mahouts were waiting to transport tourists up the stone causeway to the entrance, four passengers to a howdah. Once this was a route for glittering processions and for enemy charges led by trumpeting, armored war elephants. We were part of a more mundane cavalcade, with bands of vendors hawking postcards and embroidered velvet bags.

In the upper courtyard a steep, narrow stairway designed to deter mounted invaders led to the public audience hall, an open-sided pavilion where the potentate heard petitions, resolved disputes, and received the homage of his people. I could visualize the maharaja glittering with jewels, sitting on a carpet sewn with pearls. He would be reclining against sumptuous bolstered cushions and puffing on his hookah, or water pipe, to inhale scented tobacco or…bhang.

A majestic gate three stories high, with vaulted alcoves, arched windows, and marble screens, separated the public area from the private section of the palace with its gardens and zenana, or women's quarters.

Until about 50 years ago, Rajasthani women of the upper castes observed purdah, never appearing in public and never before a man who was not a husband or a close relative. They lived their lives cloistered within the zenana of the palace or house. If they ventured outside, they traveled veiled, keeping a purdah, literally a "curtain," to shield themselves from the eyes of strangers.

Led by our guide, we prowled a rabbit warren of rooms and a maze of terraces,

*One of a troop of langur monkeys romping where royals once resided pauses on a wall of the Amer Palace.*

courtyards, and narrow corridors designed to keep an enemy force down to single file.

It was not defense but the romantic Rajput soul that inspired the marvelously extravagant chamber we entered next—all dazzle and glitter, with stained glass inlays on the walls and mirror mosaics on the ceiling. I felt as if I were standing inside a giant jewel box. Such mirrored rooms, called *sheesh mahals*, are features of many Rajput palaces. When our guide closed the door, the mirror chips set at all angles overhead turned a single flickering candle into a thousand images shining like the spangle of stars on a desert night.

"Keep in mind, the rooms were meant to be seen while seated on very low divans, reclining against a bolster. Palaces contained very little furniture until the princes started copying the British drawing rooms in Bombay, Calcutta, and New Delhi," said Tripti Pandey, a resourceful young editor on the staff of Rajasthan's Tourism Development Corporation.

"In the early days, the palaces were mostly furnished with wall hangings and carpets. There were just some carved wooden chests and a few silver or ivory platforms cushioned with mattresses," Tripti explained over lunch at the Rambagh Palace in Jaipur. A lavish buffet, including curries, warm, crispy Indian flatbreads,

conferring with a palmist, and watching folk dancers perform under the stars. Rambagh was one of Rajasthan's first palaces to be converted into a hotel.

In 1940 Jai's first and second wives were joined at Rambagh by a third wife, the stunning Gayatri Devi. Like the others, she was a princess in her own right, but she had been educated in Europe, played tennis, rode well, and shot her first panther at the age of 12. She also appeared on lists of the world's most beautiful women. In 1962, when she ran for India's parliament, some villagers walked as far as 50 miles to hear her speak, and she was elected by the largest majority won by any candidate running for election in any democratic country in the world.

But when Gayatri Devi arrived in Jaipur the purdah system was still prevalent. On her first visit to the City Palace, where state functions took place, she traveled in a purdah car, with curtains covering the rear windows and separating the driver from the passenger seats. Jai led her through the City Palace's many public courtyards and halls, which, as she puts it, "I would never have been allowed to see alone because they were all on the men's side of the palace."

There is little evidence of purdah in the City Palace today, but it is still the scene of considerable pomp and circumstance when the people gather to greet Bhawani Singh, Jai's eldest son and the man born to rule Jaipur. He is still known as maharaja, although, strictly speaking, he is plain mister, or in his case, plain brigadier. He is also the Indian ambassador to Brunei. The titles, privileges, and allowances of the maharajas were abolished in 1971, when a constitutional amendment deprived them of honors and income. However, it did not wipe out their prestige and influence and their capacity to intimidate bureaucrats. It also

and tandoori chicken, marinated and baked to tenderness in a tandoor, or clay oven, awaited train passengers in the sprawling, white, 19th-century building.

*U*ntil 1956 Rambagh had been the home of the polo-playing Maharaja Man Singh II, "Jai." He took London by storm in the 1930s with his good looks and charm, his 40 polo ponies, their 40 grooms, and his winning team of polo-playing princes. Today the palace is a luxury hotel set amid formal English gardens. Guests can enjoy such princely pleasures as massages,

*Pillared arches of marble and sandstone decorate the Diwan-i-am, or public meeting hall, in the Amer Palace.*

*Dancer's costume becomes a blur as she whirls with clay pots balanced on her head at Jaipur's Nahargarh Fort.*

did not alter the special relationship that existed between these rulers and their subjects. The widowed Gayatri Devi, stepmother of Bhawani Singh, describes it as a "blend of concern, intimacy, and respect."

Bhawani Singh, known widely as Bubbles because the palace fountains flowed with champagne to celebrate his birth, resides in the Chandra Mahal, or Moon Palace, an airy, elegant structure with tier upon tier of balconies. It is part of the City Palace complex, which has 1,500 rooms filled with treasures. Many of these interconnected pavilions, chambers, and audience halls are open to the public, and one can easily spend a day amid the heirlooms and bric-a-brac of a great dynasty.

Another legacy from Jaipur's past thrives in the streets and lanes where jewelers fashion the intricately wrought *meenakari* jewelry—a glittering inlay of glass, mirror, and semi-precious stones—for which Jaipur is famous. The high Indian regard for jewelry perhaps reaches its zenith in Rajasthan. There are ornaments for the neck, arms, hands, ears, feet, ankles, waist, navel, nose, and forehead. And for the eyebrows there are arcs of diamonds looped over the ears with hooks.

"There are 200,000 silversmiths, goldsmiths, and workers cutting and polishing gemstones in Jaipur, following skills passed on from father to son," said Ummed Singh, a dapper guide who comes from a family of Thakurs—the chieftains or barons in the Rajput feudal society. As in feudal Europe, this hierarchy of powerful nobles provided the king with forces for his army and a retinue for his court.

"We also have to accommodate to changing times," said Ummed as we strolled down the street. "The royal family put shutters on their stables and rented the spaces out to craftsmen and tradesmen. We did the same with our city mansion," said Ummed, leading me to a large room with bales of plastic pipes stacked against the delicate wall paintings.

The reception salon had been turned over to a wholesale distributor—after removing its crystal chandelier. The second floor contained gem factories, where

*Women bring gifts to the bride's house in Jaipur on the wedding day of Shruti Kumari and Ajit Singhji.*

*A princess by lineage, the bride wears red.*

rubies, emeralds, and sapphires from all over the world are cut and polished on hand-turned wheels.

It has been said that God created maharajas so that mankind could have a spectacle of jewels and marble palaces. Their kingdoms have also been the stage for episodes of self-sacrifice and heroism that have engendered deep feelings of national pride. No princely state represents that noble tradition better than Mewar, the early capital of which was Chittorgarh—also known as Chittor—the next destination of our train.

For Indians, the mere name Chittor summons associations of warriors fighting to the death in the saffron robes of martyrdom and of their wives casting themselves into flames in mass suicide, known as *jauhar*. The story of Chittor lives on in ballads, in legends, in history books, and in

*Resplendent bridegroom arrives on an elephant.*

the memories of the people as the symbol of Hindu courage and resistance.

Chittor was a stronghold of the Sisodia dynasty from the middle of the 8th to the middle of the 16th century. Of all the Rajput clans, its warriors most fiercely fought the Muslim invaders, galloping into battle against overwhelming odds to protect their honor and their Hindu religion. In its long and bloody history, the fort fell three times in the face of overwhelming imperial forces.

As we entered the site, it was evident from the ruined palaces and temples that Chittor has suffered from time as well as from deliberate destruction. A miracle of survival is the nine-story Tower of Victory, erected in the mid-15th century and encircled with sculpture from top to bottom. Its profusion of dynamic figures provides an illustrated catalog of the Hindu pantheon of gods.

Off to another side is a 19th-century re-creation of the small, rectangular pavilion of Padmini, a legendary 13th-century beauty. According to folklore, Alauddin Khalji, the Afghan sultan in Delhi, promised to lift his siege of Chittor in 1303 for a glimpse of Queen Padmini. His intention was probably to look at the fort's inner defenses. The Rajputs reluctantly agreed to allow the sultan to view Padmini's reflec-

tion in a mirror. As the story goes, seeing her beauty made Alauddin even more determined to have Padmini in his harem. The combat and the siege were resumed.

The Rajputs held out valiantly, but they anticipated defeat. Rather than allow themselves to be captured, Padmini and every woman in the fort, some 13,000, dressed in their finest saris and immolated themselves in a vast funeral pyre. Then the men, with the ashes of the fire smeared on their foreheads and wearing the yellow robes of martyrdom, went down to the plains and battled to the death.

Alauddin entered an empty city, which, in his frustration, he ruthlessly destroyed. Some 20 years later Chittor was

*Plumed aigrette on groom's turban symbolizes royalty.*

*Bride and groom sit before a sacred fire under the golden wedding* mandap, *or canopy.*

recovered by the Sisodias, rebuilt, and defended for 200 years more. It was sacked again in 1535, but swiftly retaken. The third and final sack came in 1567, and Chittor never again served as Mewar's capital.

By ten in the morning we were en route to Udaipur, a city on the shores of Lake Pichola, where Udai Singh, heir to the Sisodia throne, transferred his capital. Here he maintained a pocket of Rajput resistance to the supremacy of the Moguls, last of the Muslim imperial dynasties. Under his successors, the Rajputs waged a guerrilla war against the Mogul troops occupying Mewar. In 1614 the last of the Rajput princes surrendered to the Moguls.

*Lake Palace Hotel seems to float on Udaipur's Lake Pichola, while the Monsoon Palace glows on the hilltop above it.*

Our first stop in Udaipur was the Lake Palace Hotel, which rises from the water like an ethereal Xanadu. On closer inspection, the Lake Palace's dreamlike allure becomes a beguiling oriental fantasy of galleries, arcades, alcoves, and interior courtyards with splashing fountains and lotus pools—a place for reverie and romance.

BLAINE HARRINGTON

In this setting Lt. Col. James Tod, the British political agent in western Rajputana from 1818 to 1822, observed the princes and their chieftains as they exchanged "the din of arms for voluptuous inactivity." In his monumental history *Annals and Antiquities of Rajasthan*, Tod records that they "slept off their noonday opiate amidst the cool breezes of the lake, wafting delicious odours from myriads of the lotus-flower...."

*M*y appointment with Princess Bhargavi Kumari Mewar took me into the private apartments within the City Palace complex. I sat with the vivacious 19-year-old in a long, semicircular room elegantly furnished in a French drawing room manner, with some unique decorating touches. About a dozen free-standing, full-size, stuffed tigers and a single leopard were artfully arranged around the room—a legacy of the princely enthusiasm for hunting. (Now it is against the law to hunt tigers in India, and former rulers are ardent wildlife conservationists.)

The princess had finished her schooling in England, and before going to college in the United States, she was devoting a year to playing polo, a fast and dangerous sport of skillful riders galloping at full tilt with mallet in hand, trying to hit a ball between goal posts. "Polo is a game India gave to the world," she explained in a smooth, low voice.

Earlier in this century Indian princes ruled the world's polo grounds. But after independence, the sport suffered a setback in India because the princely states were no longer able to finance this expensive indulgence. Costs mount up because each player needs five horses to get through a game one for each chukker, or quarter, plus one

103

*Fortified city of Jaisalmer once prospered as a crossroads for caravan trade routes.*

*Attendants pose with vintage* Palace *locomotive.*

in reserve. It generally takes two years to train a horse for the quick starts and stops of polo, and the animal's best playing years are over by the time it is eight.

"Polo survived in the country only because of the army's patronage. Now my father is helping to infuse new life in the old tradition by sponsoring the first civilian team to emerge since Independence."

As part of the project her father also breeds polo ponies, mating the local, curly-eared Mewari horse with Thoroughbreds. The stables with about 50 horses are at Shikarbadi, the former royal hunting lodge set in a small wildlife preserve just three miles from Udaipur. Like many royal residences, it has also been converted into a hotel, for the maharajas started running short of money soon after 1947, when they lost the right to collect taxes. After 1971 they were seriously short of money because they also lost their privy purse, a tax-free stipend that had been part of the accession agreements.

The *Palace on Wheel*'s overnight stay in Udaipur allowed us to accept an invitation to Shikarbadi. In the morning Sarah and I were picked up by the princess's father,

Arvind Singh Mewar, who was driving a white Mercedes. His white beard was combed with a part in the center and brushed outward and upward, in the style of his clan. He wore a casual, zippered jacket with a natty scarf. Mewar is the head of a family that has reigned for more than 1,400 years in unbroken succession—since A.D. 566.

But there were some bad apples on his tree. Take Bhim Singh, who ruled from 1778 to 1828. When the houses of both Jaipur and Jodhpur threatened to go to war for the hand in marriage of his beautiful teenage daughter Krishna Kumari, it was decreed the princess must die in order to avert the disaster of an invasion.

Overcome with remorse after her death, Bhim Singh dedicated the Krishna Vilas apartments in the City Palace to her

*Private compartment in 1980s* Palace on Wheels.

*Cheerful crowd of children greets tourists through the window of a lounge car during a brief halt.*

memory, decorating the rooms with Rajput and Mogul paintings. Like many rulers of Mewar, Bhim Singh was a great patron of miniature painting; he assembled collections of these exquisitely detailed works, which take as their subjects scenes of court life and episodes from the great Hindu epics.

Today tourists who swoop in and out of shops are the patrons. More than 2,000 artists in Udaipur, sons and grandsons of painters, work for these capricious clients. Usually the paintings take shape in assembly line fashion, as artists sit cross-legged on the floors of workshops, surrounded by worn art books, drawing and redrawing the lost splendors of Rajput royal life. One measure of their work is how successfully they capture all the minute details in the originals. A painting of an elephant in flat gray paint may sell for 60 rupees, or two dollars. Adding a thousand dots to create the textured, realistic look of elephant hide, as in the original painting, may raise the price to perhaps 200 rupees.

Back in the train, most passengers were exhibiting their purchases—block prints and tie-dyed textiles, embroidered woollen shawls, ceramics, papier-mâché ware, and silver jewelry. And postcards, for the 21-hour ride from Udaipur to Jaisalmer would allow plenty of time to write home.

**E**n route, the train crossed the Aravalli Range, which separates the more fertile eastern Rajasthan from the Great Indian Desert in the west. Next morning we rolled across a monochromatic landscape of yellow bunchgrasses, sand, gravel, and an occasional thorn tree. People in vivid raiment provided a dramatic counterpoint to their drab surroundings: men's turbans in cerise, yellow, pink, and purple;

women dressed in combinations of orange, violet, magenta, and scarlet fabrics, decorated with sequins, glitter, or tiny mirrors.

From a distance the fort of Jaisalmer rises from the golden sands like a fantastic mirage, satisfying the cravings of even the most incurable romantic. But for invaders the citadel was an unwelcoming place. The series of gates guarding entry to the fort have huge spikes, so that elephants could not be used to batter them down. The battlements have vents for pouring hot oil on anyone attempting to scale the walls. Stone cannonballs still litter the ramp, where

*Maharaja of Jodhpur Gaj Singh II relaxes in the private wing of Umaid Bhawan Palace, now a hotel.*

they had been cast down on enemies.

But commerce, not war, gave the city its identity. Founded in 1156, the fort controlled an important way station on the caravan routes linking Asia and the Mediterranean and gave the Bhatti clan of Rajputs the power to tax a major trade crossroads of the medieval world. Jaisalmer and its merchants became rich; the prosperity lasted until the need for overland routes was circumvented by the British ports at Bombay and Calcutta and the opening in 1869 of the Suez Canal.

Paved roads, railroads, and electricity bypassed Jaisalmer until the late 1960s, leaving it isolated from the changing world. Its population declined. But once the city became accessible and the world discovered its charm, a tourist boom began and has revived the economy. Some 4,000 people live within the walls of the old city and another 12,000 in the area just outside.

Cobbled lanes and dirt alleyways twist and turn past houses with intricately carved facades and balconies. Even the more modest homes may be decorated with examples of the stone carver's art. But it is the extravagantly ornate *havelis*, or

# Kingdom of the Maharajas
## Jewels and Marble Palaces

*Fateh Singh of Mewar ruled 1885-1930.*

At the time of Independence, in 1947, there were 565 native princely states in India, varying in size from more than 80,000 square miles to holdings of less than one square mile. Some of the maharajas, or great kings, earned reputations for extravagance and eccentricity with their sumptuous palaces, their lavish tiger shoots supplied with champagne and caviar, and their fleets of luxury motor cars upholstered in satins, velvets, and brocades. One ruler celebrated the mating of his favorite dog with an opulent wedding attended by more than 700 guests from all over India.

Some maharajas were notorious playboys. Take the 35th in the ruling dynasty of Marwar, who at 18 immersed himself in bacchanalian revelry where dancing girls swooned with exhaustion at parties that lasted for days. Warned by his doctor he would die within three years, Maharaja Sumer Singh replied, laughing: "You are wrong, I will rule for six, for I will turn night into day." He died at 21.

Other potentates were exceedingly pious. Madho Singh of Jaipur would neither drink nor bathe in water from any other source than the holy Ganges River. On his trip to England in 1902 to attend the coronation of Edward VII, he carried his water supply in two immense silver water urns that were five feet high and weighed 680 pounds each.

Still other maharajas were responsible administrators, genuinely concerned with the welfare of their people. For example, Ganga Singh, the remarkable 21st ruler of Bikaner, built schools, hospitals, railways, and an 89-mile canal that irrigated a thousand square miles of his desert state. By the end of his 56-year reign in 1943, he had transformed Bikaner from a feudal kingdom into a progressive state.

The spectacle the maharajas presented to the world came to an end in 1971, when the princes were stripped of the titles, privileges, and stipends, or privy purses, granted to them under the terms of accession to India. However, the splendor and romance of that vanished world lingers on in the fairy tale citadels and palaces that serve now as hotels or museums.

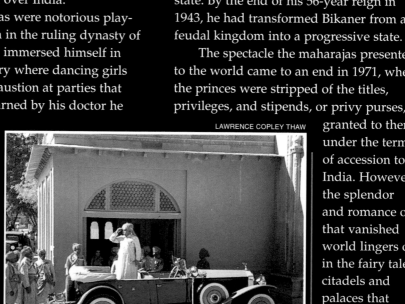

*Maharaja Ganga Singh salutes from his Rolls Royce in 1940.*

mansions, that are the pride of Jaisalmer and exhibit the virtuoso skills of the local artisans. I stood fascinated before the haveli of the jeweler-merchant Patwon. Every pillar, every bracket and balcony was pierced with floral or geometric designs of breathtaking craftsmanship. Every window was screened with filigreed stone. Almost no surface was untouched by skilled hands that turned stone into lace.

"Do you want a carpet? I know a good place," said a slender young man, walking in step beside me.

"How about a shawl or a wall hanging? Not buy, just looking. Come, just look. My friend will give you a good price."

At times the spiel of the street touts intruded on the ambiance of the old city. But for the most part, I was undisturbed as I wandered streets where nanny goats nursed their kids. Through open doors I caught glimpses of domestic scenes: a mother braiding her daughter's long hair, a woman slapping a ball of dough into a flat pancake to fry into a soft, crispy *paratha*.

In the market area, vendors sitting cross-legged on the ground weighed out green beans and carrots, with bangles jingling on their arms. At one of the pigeonhole shops a tailor pedaled at a treadle sewing machine. At a sweetmeat shop, round *jalebis* sizzled in deep oil.

In the afternoon, *Palace* passengers were driven to an area of sand dunes, for the spectacle of sunset and an evening of folk music and dance. Starting with the staccato beat of drums, the dancers stamped and swiveled their feet, swaying and stepping in a jingle of ankle bells to the lively tune played by the harmonium and stringed *sarangi*. Little is altered by the fact that the two sultry girls turned out to be boys in disguise, a specialty of members of professional entertainers called Bhawais. They are also noted for a dance nimbly executed while balancing seven clay pots on the head.

Our next stop, Jodhpur, had been the

*Smoke marked the* Palace's *progress across Rajasthan in 1983, before diesel engines replaced the iron horse.*

*Carvings of handprints in Jodhpur honor widows who cast themselves on their husbands' funeral pyres.*

capital of the state of Marwar, largest of Rajasthan's princely states. In the 1930s, when the heir to its throne, Hanwant Singh, went off to Mayo College, the princes' preparatory school established by the British in Ajmer, he took a couple of cars, a few horses, some guns, and his servants, including a barber and a tailor.

At the school the young men were trained in what a British educator once listed as essential skills for an Indian prince: "the speaking of faultless English, possesing [sic] excellent table manners, and playing good cricket."

But as author of the *House of Marwar*, Dhananajaya Singh, points out, the tall, sturdy Hanwant Singh did not turn out to be "the patronising English colonel's 'beau ideal of a native prince.'" He succeeded to the throne at age 24 on the eve of India's Independence—August 15, 1947.

Those were turbulent times, for the partition of the subcontinent into India and Pakistan turned Hindu and Muslim against each other and unleashed a rampage of violence. But the young maharaja kept Marwar, which bordered on Pakistan, free of bloodshed. Marwar was one of the last states to accede to India before the country became a republic in 1950. As part of the maharaja's negotiated agreement, the 15th-century fort of Meherangarh, the ancestral home of the Rathore dynasty, remains family property. Now it is run privately as a museum by a trust settled by the maharaja. An oriental fantasy on the heights, with graceful balconies overhanging mighty battlements, the royal aerie crowns a rocky crag some 400 feet above the city.

When Rudyard Kipling saw it in the

*Young folk dancer performs below Jodhpur's fort as a musician plays the* ravanahatta, *a stringed instrument.*

late 1880s, he thought only giants could have made it. About entering the fort, he wrote, "It would be a week's work...to describe the bewildering multiplicity of courts and ranges of rooms...."

As for the furnishings: "Dresden China snuff-boxes, mechanical engines, electro-plated fish-slicers, musical boxes, and gilt blown-glass Christmas-tree balls do not go well with the splendours of a Palace that might have been built by Titans and coloured by the morning sun. But there are excuses to be made for Kings who have no fighting to do." Kipling, however, omitted mention of the gorgeous carpets, the ornate elephant howdahs, the array of musical instruments, elaborate cradles and palan-quins, and the magnificent wall mosaics of stained glass and semiprecious stones set in gold filigree.

I asked Gaj Singh II, the 38th Rathore, what *he* particularly treasures among the collections at Meherangarh. "One of my favorites is a large, luxurious, red velvet

*Winding lanes of old Jodhpur house traditional artisans as well as traders dealing in cattle, camels, and cotton.*

and gold-brocaded tent that belonged to one of the Mogul emperors. Actually, it is not on exhibit because it was deteriorating in the sunlight," said the maharaja in a soft British accent that reflects rather than proclaims his education at Eton and Oxford. "Among the more modern things, I'm fond of a 1925 convertible Rolls Royce. It's very sporty looking, with a body specially built with more chrome on it."

We were sitting on an enclosed veranda overlooking the formal lawns of the grandiose Umaid Bhawan Palace, completed in 1943. In a style reminiscent of art deco, with an Indo-colonial flavor, the vast pink palace has a central dome and formal symmetry that give it the air of a stately municipal building. It looks as if parliament might be in session in a chamber somewhere down its long marble hallways.

But in the private sitting room next to the veranda, the style was more relaxed. A large coffee table was covered with a chess set, glossy magazines, and the videos

*Schindler's List*, *Dr. Zhivago*, *Cabaret*, and *Yoga in Daily Life*. Chinese side tables, a framed Chinese embroidery, and a large screen contrasted with the English country house look. India was present in the imposing portraits of Gaj Singh's ancestors and a subtle aroma of incense.

When he completed his education in England at age 23 and returned to a tumultuous reception in Jodhpur, Gai Singh also faced complicated financial difficulties.

"Many of the properties had been sold to the Indian government or were lost by default," he explained. "Turning part of Umaid Bhawan into a hotel was a very difficult decision for me." He rejected a more profitable deal with a hotel chain that would have required replacing hundreds of retainers on the staff with professionals. "How could I abandon these people who have served my family for generations?"

A man of many interests and involvements, Gaj Singh is chairman of this, patron of that, managing trustee, and

*Blue exterior of an adobe house in Jodhpur indicates the high-caste Braman status of the residents.*

convener, but perhaps his most respected form of address is "Bapji," honored father. In Jodhpur it is the maharaja's traditional title, and it is what Gaj Singh is still affectionately called by his people.

Our departure came too soon. In the afternoon we boarded the train for the 19-hour ride to Bikaner, home of India's Bikaner Camel Corps, reputed to be the most flamboyant military unit of modern times. The city is also the home of Bhawal Khan's dancing camels, which bob on three legs to the beat of a drum while twirling the other leg. Bikaner was a meeting place for desert traders on the old caravan route from Central Asia when it was captured in the 1480s by Bika, one of the many sons of the founder of Jodhpur.

Bikaner's Junagadh Fort, with its forbidding gray-pink sandstone exterior, was constructed between 1588 and 1593. But over the course of the next 300 years, it grew into an immense palace complex with all the Rajput taste for grandeur.

One chamber we visited stands out as distinctly different. Its ceiling was painted with swollen storm clouds. Dark, jagged streaks tracked bolts of lightning on the pale walls to conjure up the rainy season. This cloud palace, our guide explained, was built to put a maharaja in a monsoon mood; he liked to play the musical ragas associated with the rains.

The hunt, or shikar, however, was the great avocation of princes. They organized lavish shoots, "roughing it" in carpeted tents with fireplaces, in camps supplied with delicacies, brandies, and champagne, and staffed with cooks who created elegant meals for banquet tables. The reloading of guns was left to liveried gun bearers.

Bikaner's dynamic Maharaja Ganga Singh made the annual sand grouse shoot at his preserve and palatial lodge at Lake Gajner one of the most sought-after events on the imperial social calendar. He also made the most of the opportunity with his British guests by combining pleasure with politics, for Ganga Singh worked tirelessly to make his kingdom a modern state.

At the 19th-century red sandstone Lallgarh Palace on the outskirts of the city, where we ate lunch, the walls attest to Ganga Singh's marksmanship—tiger skins, mounted heads of black buck and *chinkara*, an elusive deer. A greater monument is the

*Marble mausoleum, the Taj Mahal in Agra pays homage to Emperor Shah Jahan's beloved wife, who died in 1631.*

89-mile-long Gang Canal, which brings water to his former desert kingdom. He also built the railways, roads, and independent court system that helped transform his kingdom into a progressive state.

Ganga Singh died in 1943, six years after his golden jubilee celebration, when, according to custom, the beloved maharaja was weighed against gold from the state's treasury, and the cash equivalent was donated to charity. The Golden Jubilee Book records: "...the jewels, and swords, and greetings...in the large durbar hall with its carved walls and ceilings. Roses and other flowers—great rarities in dry Bikaner —were showered on the Maharaja...while women sang songs of rejoicing."

Such gorgeous spectacles will not return to Bikaner. A way of life dazzling and audacious enough to take one's breath away is gone, its memory preserved in the romantic beauty of its fortress-palaces.

As we boarded the train in the darkening afternoon, the city and palaces of Bikaner receded from view. But my journey, like the candle in the Sheesh Mahal at Amer, has ignited a thousand shimmering images to carry with me.

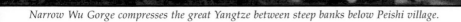

# Cruising up the Mighty
# Yangtze River

by Elisabeth B. Booz

Photographs by George Steinmetz

*Narrow Wu Gorge compresses the great Yangtze between steep banks below Peishi village.*

*Equally at home in 13 river ports, a Yangtze deckhand perches on his boat's bollards to enjoy a bowl of rice.*

**W**here on earth am I? It is after midnight. I'm standing, wet and weary, at an 18th-floor window in a hotel with an unpronounceable name—the Qingchuan. I'm supposed to be in Wuhan, a great city straddling the Yangtze River in the center of China. But I'm not sure.

Beyond the rain-drenched window I see…nothing. Empty blackness. A line of far-off, twinkling lights reassures me that I haven't suddenly gone blind. I must be way out in the countryside somewhere.

My great journey up the Yangtze River is not starting well. No river. Also no boat.

This morning, during a brief layover in Hong Kong, I learned that my new, German-built, Chinese-run, luxury cruise boat, the *Princess Sheena*, had run aground somewhere up the Yangtze. My travel agent had put me instead on the refurbished *Qiao Feng*, which would be just as —well, almost as—satisfactory, he said.

I arrived at Wuhan's airport, hours behind schedule, during a spectacular spring thunderstorm. A car trip through torrential rain and darkness brought me to the courtyard of a cavernous, apparently deserted hotel. A sleepy clerk in a powder blue uniform led me to this room.

Suddenly, out my window, a flash of lightning cracks the sky. In one dazzling moment I know where I am.

The great Yangtze stretches out directly below me, the distant line of lights marking the far shore. Dark shapes of countless sleeping ships and barges etch the bright surface. Then the scene goes black.

My hotel is right on the riverbank.

A hundred years ago another curious woman came to explore the Yangtze. Isabella Bird was one of the best known and most intrepid of Victorian England's women travelers. Her books enthralled a wide public, for she could not resist the romance of discovery.

China, little known at that time, was being drawn against its will into Britain's worldwide commercial orbit. Off went Isabella, undaunted by her 64 years. She recounted such a remarkable, often hair-raising, journey into the heart of China by way of its magnificent, merciless river that I decided to follow her. Now I want to find out if the 20th century and 46 years of communism have tamed the Yangtze.

I wake up at daylight and run to the window. The great river is still there, the color of milky tea, over half a mile wide and dotted clear across with boats. Low, ragged clouds scud across the sky. Clusters of barges maneuver around the mouth of the Han River on my left, and a load of trash dumped from a cabin window is snatched away by the current in seconds.

A massive, double-tiered bridge spans the river on concrete piers. I'm looking at the first bridge ever to span the Yangtze— built under Mao Zedong in 1957. Cars shuttle nonstop on top; trains charge across below them. But the Wuhan metropolitan area has more than six million people. Most of them cross the river on ferryboats. Humans and bicycles flow in a steady stream to the floating docks that line the riverbank.

A tiny figure in the water, looking no bigger than a fly, catches my eye. I reach for my binoculars. A lone fisherman is battling the current, up to his waist in swirling, muddy water. An inner tube attached to his body holds his fishing gear. The size of that miniature fisherman

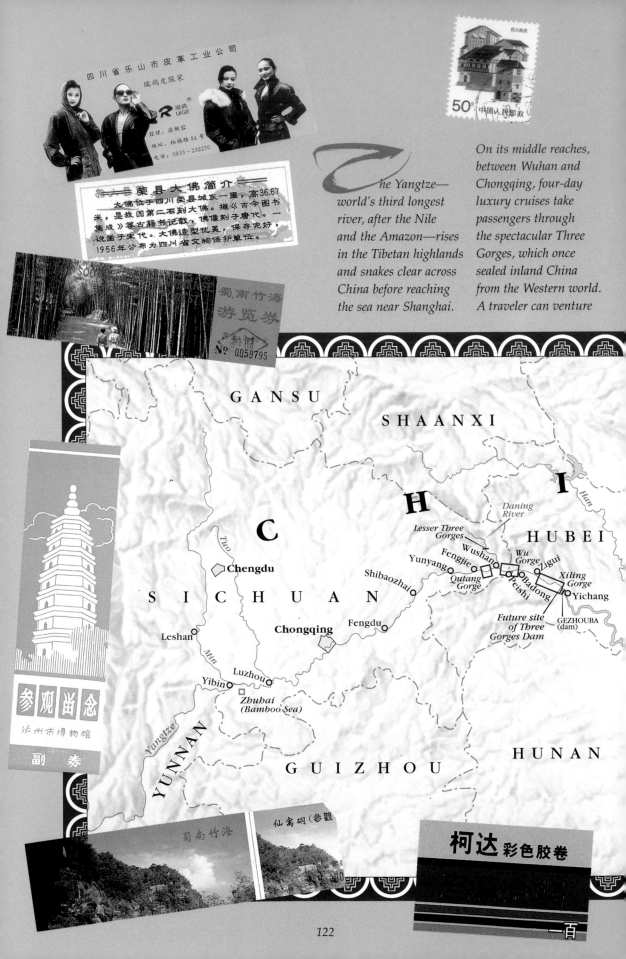

四川省乐山市皮革工业公司

瑞鸽皮服装

R 瑞鸽 UIGE

经理：梁新容
地址：杨扬路84号
电话：0833—232270

百川民居

50 中国人民邮政

荣县大佛简介

大佛位于四川荣县城东一里，高36.67
米，是我国第二石刻大佛。据《古今图书
集成》等古籍书记载，佛像刻于唐代。一
说凿于宋代。大佛造型优美，保存完好，
1956年公布为四川省文物保护单位。

蜀南竹海
游览券

No. 0059795

参观留念

泸州市博物馆

副 券

*he Yangtze—
world's third longest
river, after the Nile
and the Amazon—rises
in the Tibetan highlands
and snakes clear across
China before reaching
the sea near Shanghai.

On its middle reaches,
between Wuhan and
Chongqing, four-day
luxury cruises take
passengers through
the spectacular Three
Gorges, which once
sealed inland China
from the Western world.
A traveler can venture

GANSU

SHAANXI

C H I

Daning
River

Lesser Three
Gorges

HUBEI

Wushan

Wu
Gorge

Zigui

Fengjie

Yunyang

Fengjie

Xiling
Gorge

Qutang
Gorge

Badong

Yichang

Peishi

Shibaozhai

Chengdu

Tuo

S I C H U A N

Future site
of Three
Gorges Dam

GEZHOUBA
(dam)

Leshan

Min

Chongqing

Fengdu

Luzhou

Yibin

Zhuhai
(Bamboo Sea)

Yangtze

YUNNAN

G U I Z H O U

HUNAN

蜀南竹海

仙寓硐(参观)

柯达彩色胶卷

10 拾圓

中國銀行
外匯兌換券

ZE 600605

一九七九年

侨丰
QIAO FENG

*farther by following the river through Sichuan Province to Yibin, the last navigable port. There the Min tributary leads to Leshan and the world's largest sitting Buddha statue.*

WISH YOU GOOD NIGHT
DON'T PUT YOUR WET CLOTHES ON LAMPSHADES, THANKS!

祝君晚安
請勿將濕衣物凉在燈罩上，謝謝！

侨丰
QIAO FENG

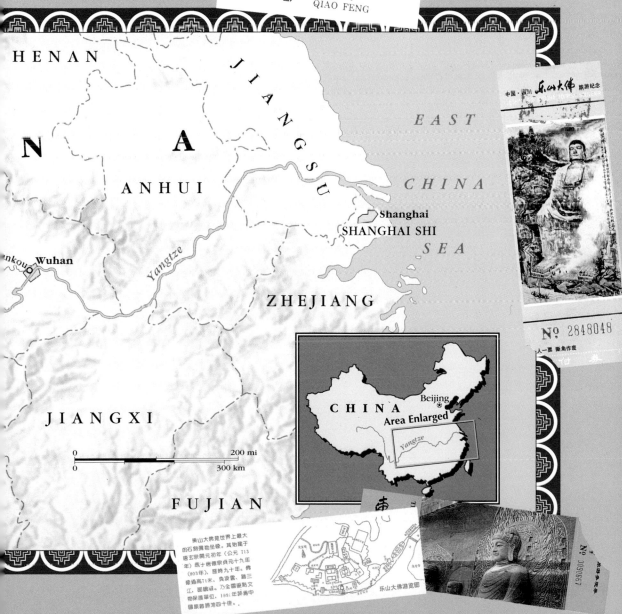

HENAN

JIANGSU

N   A

ANHUI

EAST

CHINA

SEA

Shanghai
SHANGHAI SHI

nkou  Wuhan

Yangtze

ZHEJIANG

JIANGXI

0                              200 mi
0                              300 km

CHINA
Beijing ⊛
Area Enlarged
Yangtze

FUJIAN

中国·四川 乐山大佛 旅游纪念

Nº 2848048

乐山大佛是世界上最大的石刻弥勒坐像。其始凿于唐玄宗开元初年（公元 713年）成十唐德宗贞元十九年（803年），历时九十年。佛像通高71米，魚凫蛮、踞三江、郎跳峰。乃全国重点文物保护单位。1991年跻身中国旅游者首选四十佳。

乐山大佛游览图

Nº 096967

*Above Yichang the Yangtze will become a vast lake created by the Three Gorges Dam, now under construction.*

suddenly hits me. This is a human being like me. Everything else in view is too big to grasp.

*China's flag flies from a riverboat's stern.*

Isabella Bird landed in Shanghai in January 1896. China had never welcomed foreigners, but Britain had forced it, through "unequal treaties," to open a few ports to foreign trade along the coast and the lower Yangtze River. There were fortunes to be made in China from tea, textiles, and opium. These "treaty ports" eventually numbered more than 30.

The British highhandedly dubbed the river the Yangtze, unaware that the Chinese only used "Yangtze" for a short section near its mouth. The river baffled the British. It was the main route to the rich, inland province of Sichuan, yet they could not get there. Three giant gorges lay a thousand miles upstream between the busy treaty port of Hankow—now spelled Hankou and absorbed into the modern city of Wuhan, where I began my journey—and Chungking, now Chongqing, Sichuan's largest city. The only foreigners to pass through the gorges had been missionaries and an occasional diplomat, risking their lives on junks that were hauled over rapids and reefs with fraying bamboo ropes harnessed to straining men known as trackers. Isabella was determined to follow the mysterious Yangtze as far as she could go. So was I.

The Chinese give two names to the Yangtze on its nearly 4,000-mile course above its mouth. The first half, cascading wildly down from its mountain source to Sichuan's plain, is called the River of Golden Sand ("Jinsha"). The second half,

*A ship enters the 1980s-era Gezhouba dam for a stair-step rise to the level of the Three Gorges.*

the Long River ("Chang Jiang"), traverses the remaining 2,000 miles of China. Its basin shelters one-third of China's population and produces about 70 percent of its rice. The Long River starts at a point deep in Sichuan where the Golden Sand joins the calmer Min River at a small city named Yibin. I set my sights on Yibin.

The Yangtze still holds mysteries. Its point of origin—21,723 feet high on the Qinghai-Tibet Plateau—was not revealed until 1976, and its exact location is still disputed. If somebody can prove that those lofty headwaters are just 36 miles longer than Chinese geographers currently say, then the Yangtze will become the second longest river in the world—longer than the Amazon, surpassed only by the Nile.

I decided to skip the first leg of Isabella's journey, from Shanghai to

*Farmer and water buffalo prepare rice fields for planting on Xiling Gorge's agriculturally diverse terraces.*

Hankou. She hated Shanghai. The English she met yawned at her interest in Chinese civilization. Isabella, in turn, deplored Britain's gunboats and its aggressive "sphere of influence." She crossed China's wide coastal plain on a British copy of a Mississippi riverboat, complete with gilded mirrors and electric lights, which she scorned. Such luxuries, Isabella felt, took all the romance out of travel.

I, too, would have found it a bad trip, though for different reasons. The coastal plain is now heavily industrialized, the river is polluted, and high dikes cut out much of the view. I would start my journey in Hankou, where Isabella's spirits rose at the first scent of adventure.

She found Hankou a bit seedy. Its glory days had been back in the 1860s, when splendid clippers like the *Cutty Sark* sailed up the Yangtze to take on tea and then race back around the tip of Africa to London. Steamships and the Suez Canal had killed them. I found ponderous colonial buildings with columned facades still standing on Hankou's waterfront, holding their own among trendy shops and bars. But in the busy port, the stately junks that once crowded the wharfs were all gone.

At dusk I board the *Qiao Feng*—an ungainly, five-story, 280-foot shoe box of a boat that draws only 6 feet of water. Unlike the sleek, stranded *Princess Sheena*, this is a typical Yangtze passenger boat. Millions of people a year travel the river in everything from ferries to fancy, foreign-run cruise boats. I rank the *Qiao Feng* between the two extremes, in the top quarter, with a distinctly local flavor.

I enter amidships into a large oval lobby with velvet sofas and potted palms. Zeng Yudong, the ship's interpreter-cum-guide, introduces himself in fluent English as "Harry," peers at me through owl-like glasses, and ushers me to my stateroom. Spacious and attractive, with a big window, it is in "super first class"—a consolation prize, I guess, for whatever unknown luxuries I am missing on the *Princess Sheena*.

In Mao Zedong's time, first class was despised as bourgeois snobbery. A ship's top accommodations were labeled second class and went down the scale to fifth class. This boat's 86 cabins start with first class and go up the scale through "super" to a couple of "super-super" (unoccupied) suites with marble bathrooms.

A blast of the ship's horn brings me up on deck as we leave our Hankou dock. I stand in the dark with the wind in my hair and a ditty of muted, nighttime river noises in my ears until we pass by the Qingchuan Hotel and under the double-tiered bridge I saw at dawn.

At breakfast, half the dining room's big round tables are empty. The cruise season is only beginning. A group of Chinese-Malaysians eats on one side and a larger group from Taiwan exchanges riotous jokes

*Shennong Stream, a Yangtze tributary, has carved gorges with cliffs a thousand feet high.*

on the other. The designated English-speaking table includes three quiet Canadian couples and myself.

A flurry of apologies erupts near the door, and we are abruptly joined by a jovial, elderly, Taiwanese-Australian and his elegant wife, who had mistakenly been seated with the rowdy Taiwanese. "Call me Sam!" he booms. The English-speaking table bursts into life.

The *Qiao Feng*'s recreational possibilities seem sparse. A fierce woman in a white

overall offers Chinese massages. Two intriguing, Rube Goldberg-style, exercise machines stand on a stair landing. When I peek under the cover of a promising little swimming pool, I find it dry and transformed into a crew member's bedroom. But the top floor has plenty to offer. Up front is a sitting area with panoramic windows and a secluded deck; in the middle is

*A boatman skillfully steers his wooden craft through dangerous currents below Shennong Stream's crags.*

a karaoke parlor with a huge TV screen, strobe lights, and a dance floor; and at the back, a gaudy piano bar with gambling tables. Entertainment for all.

For healthy workouts, I join Call-Me-Sam and his wife, Nancy, on the top deck for daily, before-breakfast, tai chi exercises. The first day, I arrive too early. Waiting by the rail, I suddenly decipher in the mist a long white boat, lying still in the current. I can just make out the letters on its side— *Princess Sheena!* By the time Sam and Nancy appear in their jogging suits, the apparition has vanished.

The couple had also been booked on the *Princess Sheena* and knew the true story. More than 400 feet long, the boat had been built in Germany for a Russian cruise company to run on the Volga River. In Russia's economic turmoil the company had collapsed, and China picked up the *Sheena* and two sister ships for tourism on the Yangtze. "She's too long and too deep!" roars Sam. "Not suitable for the Yangtze!"

At midmorning we reach Yichang, at the mouth of Xiling Gorge. Boats and barges have quadrupled in number. Ahead looms Gezhouba, a massive 230-foot dam. Completed in 1988, it was China's first attempt to harness the formidable Yangtze for hydroelectric power and flood control.

*I*sabella Bird reached Yichang on an American-built stern-wheeler crowded with Chinese and a handful of missionaries. Hostile peasants on shore shrieked, "Foreign devils!" and pelted them with mud. Her steamer turned back to Hankou, and passengers prepared to board junks at a place where the *Qiao Feng* is now sailing placidly into the largest of three locks. It takes us hardly ten minutes to rise 82 feet to the water level of the Three Gorges.

I run forward to get my first glimpse and stop dead. There is no gorge—only a ravaged landscape that looks like a huge, hideous, strip mine. Raw, scarred earth, tin-roofed buildings, bulldozers, cranes, as far as the eye can see.

A cliff on the south shore bears eight giant Chinese characters that Harry reads aloud: "Construction of Three Gorges Dam—Development of Yangtze River." Puffs of dynamited debris burst out from the cliff face and ornament the slogan like a bouquet of dead, gray flowers.

This is the site of what will be the world's largest hydroelectric system. The Gezhouba, which we have just passed, will be a midget beside it. The Three Gorges Dam—60 feet higher than the Grand

Coulee Dam and 2,000 feet longer—will block the Yangtze and create an elongated lake 372 miles long. More than 300 towns and villages will drown in its depths. The Three Gorges will disappear. More than a million people will need new homes. It boggles my mind.

I am in a sad mood as we enter Xiling,

*A miner hauls a loaded coal sled near Badong.*

the longest of the Three Gorges, soon to become a mere memory. It is, in fact, a 47-mile complex of seven smaller gorges, each with its own character. Stratified rock formations have given rise to fantastic names—Yellow Cat Gorge, Military Books and Precious Sword Gorge, Ox Liver and Horse Lungs Gorge. Harry points them out

*Beyond a wild landscape of eroded limestone near Wu Gorge, a painted gateway leads to cultivated fields.*

*A hen shares a farmer's living room with portraits of Communist luminaries in remote Peishi.*

*Tourists relax on board in an elegant cocktail lounge.*

as the river narrows and the current eddies past our ship at a swirling eight miles an hour.

This lowest of the Three Gorges was once the most feared by boatmen, for its riverbed is shaped like a submerged roller coaster. At the long, precipitous New Rapids, named after a landslide in the 16th century, extra trackers had to be harnessed to a junk's arm-thick hawsers. Disembarked passengers were obliged to walk a steep mountain track past the dreaded White Bone Pagoda, which was reputedly built with the bleached bones of people who had perished there.

Isabella hired a flat-bottomed houseboat in Yichang, with 16 trackers or oarsmen, as circumstances required. She observed the river and the shore diligently from its deck, with binoculars at hand. But she scrambled ashore at the infamous New Rapids. Her little boat needed 70 men to haul it up the roiling, stair-step shoals. Could Europeans ever hope to bring steamships up the Yangtze to Sichuan?

*A*rchibald Little, a flamboyant English entrepreneur, was the first to try. He got a small steamer to Chungking (Chongqing) in 1898—but trackers were needed to pull it through the gorges. In

*Luxury ships transport tourists on the Yangtze ten months a year, bringing precious foreign currency into China.*

134

*Local boats offer cheap tickets to passengers between Wuhan and Chongqing, with stops at many small ports.*

1900 he succeeded in winching a 180-foot side-wheeler over the rapids. But a bigger German boat that followed, hoping to horn in on the opening of Sichuan, struck a reef in Xiling Gorge and sank. "It blocked river traffic for nine years," exclaimed Harry, in an outraged tone.

The captain of Archibald Little's boats was a modest man named Cornell Plant who knew more about the river than his boss did. When Little died, Plant built a powerful tug, financed by Chinese investors, and lashed it to a barge specially designed to carry both cargo and passengers. It worked so well that in 1909 he started a regular service between Yichang and Chongqing, training all the river pilots himself. Other steamship companies followed his lead. When Cornell Plant retired to a bungalow overlooking the New Rapids, ships braving the shoals would toot their horns and watch for a wave of the old riverman's handkerchief.

A monument was erected there after his death. I wonder if it survived the Cultural Revolution of the 1960s. But when I ask Harry to point out the New Rapids,

he looks puzzled. "Oh," he says, as light dawns. "You mean the Green Shore! It's along here." Mao Zedong dredged and dynamited the worst hazards of the Three Gorges in the 1950s, eliminating the New Rapids. But Plant's little obelisk still stands on a hill above.

At the end of Xiling Gorge, we dock at Zigui, home of a revered poet whose drowning suicide in 278 B.C. gave rise to China's annual Dragon Boat Festival. Bessie Shen, a sprightly widow with the Malaysian group, tells me she always celebrates the festival by eating special sticky rice cakes to recall the poet's noble character. "I think it's very good to remember these ancient things about China," she explains. Mrs. Shen—her formal British education in Malacca precluded our using first names—describes herself as "Overseas Chinese." She has visited China before but this time has chosen the Yangtze trip, she says, to get a feel for the "real China" that lies beyond the cities and museums.

Zigui is a town of steps, ascending a small mountain in tiers. Doomed to drown, it is reaping every profit it can. Each stone

*A broad sweep of river greets a Yangtze pilot as he steers beyond Qutang Gorge to Shibaozhai.*

*New styles for China's city dwellers include trendy international clothes.*

*Sedan chairs, banned in China for decades as demeaning, make a comeback at Wushan to carry tourists over mud.*

step has a smiling salesperson displaying hats, back scratchers, coins, carvings, tablecloths, embroidery, and knickknacks. Up, up, up. The poet's temple with curly cornered roofs will soon be moved downstream stone by stone to be rebuilt and preserved near Yichang.

On the floating dock, a homemade theater with folding chairs presents Zigui's local talent. Pretty girls sing and dance in glittery costumes. But the final act moves me. It is a boatman's dance, with stamping feet and eerie shouts, performed by old men. Isabella wrote, "If tracking and sailing are both impossible, the trackers propel the junk with great oars, each worked by two men, twenty at a side, who face forward and mark time with a combined stamp and wild chant." Here they are, grandfathers born in that time of peril, evoking a terrible reality. They lend dignity to the little makeshift theater.

The *Qiao Feng* zigzags against the river's blackened south bank. Laborers lug huge baskets of coal down a vertical slope to open barges. High above them, tiny figures are constructing new buildings and a road above the future waterline. Perhaps life there will be better for coal miners.

The cliffs of sunless Wu Gorge—also known as Witches Gorge—loom close. Twelve peaks, six on each side, are wrapped in eternal clouds, drenched in myth and fairy tale. They look bleak and scary to me. Lion Peak, Dragon's Spine. The water around us is filled with sinister, racing crosscurrents and flattened, evil-looking whirlpools. Romance is spiced with danger.

"Look! Look!" shouts Harry. The mist has shifted, momentarily revealing Goddess Peak, the highest summit. A thousand feet above us, a small rock pinnacle shaped like a draped maiden stands out clearly—a goddess turned to stone for defying her father and falling in love with a mortal emperor.

The *Qiao Feng*'s horn bleats as if it's stuck. Two sampans are directly in our

# Isabella Bird

*Isabella Bird posed in the 1890s in silken Manchu robes fit for the Empress of China.*

*I*sabella Bird was the best known of that remarkable breed, the Victorian woman traveler. Yet she started late in life.

Born in 1831, the daughter of an English clergyman, she grew up a semi-invalid, with a chronic spine ailment, devoting her time to worthy causes between bouts of depression. She seemed the least likely person to become an explorer, a best-selling author, and the first woman to be elected a fellow of the Royal Geographical Society.

She began to blossom at the age of 41, when a doctor prescribed the classic remedy of that era for ailing gentlewomen—a long sea voyage.

The short, dowdy spinster left her sister Henrietta and sailed to Australia. But that did not cure her. It took a full-blown Pacific typhoon on her return trip to restore her health. Isabella's strength surged back as she faced real danger on her foundering paddle wheeler. Instead of going home, she disembarked at the Sandwich Islands —today's Hawaii.

The exotic Polynesian kingdom inspired her. She explored the islands and climbed volcanoes. When her back ached from riding sidesaddle, she felt free to straddle a Mexican saddle, wearing dainty frilled trousers. For, as she wrote, "Travellers are privileged to do the most improper things with perfect propriety, that is one charm of travelling."

Voluminous letters to Henrietta were the basis of Isabella's widely read *Six Months in the Sandwich Islands,* published in 1875.

Crossing America, Isabella discovered Colorado— "no region for tourists and women." She rode 800 miles through the wild, rugged Rockies, living with hunters and trappers, and was charmed by Mountain Jim, a well-read, one-eyed desperado "whom any woman might love but no sane woman would marry." With personal details edited out, *A Lady's Life in the Rocky Mountains* received rave reviews and went through eight editions.

Home in Edinburgh, Isabella fell ill again. Dr. John Bishop, her friend and physician, offered her diversions, but in 1878 Isabella headed toward Japan. In blooming health she reached the remote haunts of the hairy Ainu aborigines.

But it was Malaya (today's Peninsular Malaysia), on her return voyage, that captivated her with its extravagant colors, elephants, and gibbons. The resulting books solidified her reputation as a brilliant observer of foreign scenes.

Henrietta's death from typhoid in 1880 left Isabella bereft. The following year, at age 50, she married Dr. Bishop, who understood her well. He said, "I have only one formidable rival in Isabella's heart, and that is the high tableland of Central Asia."

# A Remarkable Breed of Traveler

Within five years, the good doctor caught an infection and died.

Isabella turned to the church, taking great interest in missionaries. She continued traveling and writing, and her reputation kept growing. On her return from India and the nation then known as Persia, she was presented to Queen Victoria and invited to dine with Prime Minister William Gladstone.

In 1896, after a visit to Korea, she sailed up the Yangtze, ostensibly to visit missionaries. But her old spirit of adventure took over. Beyond the river's hazardous gorges, she set out into Tibet's unknown border regions, nearly losing her life. Her book *The Yangtze Valley and Beyond* opened England's eyes to civilizations unrecorded by its empire builders.

Unstopped by advancing years, Isabella visited Morocco in 1901. She died in Edinburgh three years later with her bags packed for a return trip to China. She had traveled where few Western women had ever been and made unimaginable places spring to life for her readers.

*In Isabella Bird's time, all shipping was hauled upstream through the Yangtze's gorges by teams of straining trackers harnessed to tow ropes by shoulder slings. Seventy men pulled Isabella's small houseboat over rapids in Xiling Gorge. A large junk often required more than 300 trackers.*

E. T. SHIELDS

*In the dry season, with river level low, temporary food stalls line the long climb from boats up to Fengjie.*

path. The larger one makes for shore, but the smaller one, its long oars straining, can make no headway against the current. Our captain's voice, booming through a bullhorn, reverberates off the cliffs. I'm frightened we'll hit the sampan. At the last minute it slips under our bow and whirls past us sideways, oars flailing, then straightens out to meet our wake head-on.

Fish hawks swoop over the water. A hundred feet above, the abandoned trackers' path is hollowed out of sheer rock like an open-sided tube, just big enough for men bent double in shoulder harnesses. River levels are painted on the cliff up to 35 meters (115 feet). We are at 4 meters (13 feet) now.

When we emerge from Witches Gorge, we are in Sichuan Province. We tie up for the night at Wushan, where the Daning River meets the Yangtze. The Daning is famed for its towering Lesser Three Gorges. Mrs. Shen tells me it has its own

tributary, the Madu, with the Mini-Three Gorges. Nobody seems able to tell me why Chinese gorges always come in threes.

Sam is convinced we will drown on the Daning. Mountains of orange life preservers appear in the lobby after dinner. The next morning Sam is already wearing his at breakfast.

In an orange swarm, we cross a floating dock and wobbly planks to a stretch of mudflats. Porters trot hopefully abreast of us, bearing bright red sedan chairs, but have no takers. I look at my mud-covered, once-white sneakers and am tempted.

On a waiting bus, the local guide's first words are, "This is Wushan. Soon the whole city will be under 56 meters [184 feet] of water." We are not allowed to forget. Yet when Mrs. Shen questions a middle-aged passerby from the bus window, he just shrugs. He is an auto mechanic, he says, and he has already received his notice to move by the year 2003. "They're building a new town over the hill." Has he endured so many upheavals that one more doesn't faze him?

*Age-old stone steps yield treasures for a young resident of Yunyang.*

Wushan's port on the Daning River is crammed with motorized sampans taking tourists to the Lesser Three Gorges. My heart sinks. But once I am moving on the clear, swift river, I ignore them.

I am miraculously transported into a world of classical Chinese painting and poetry. Sheer cliffs, a thousand feet high, look as though they have been laid in with a delicate brush and ink. Birds dart about graceful clumps of bamboo, and fishermen pole slender wooden boats shaped like willow leaves through the foaming rapids. I share Mrs. Shen's delight in the pure beauty of it.

Only when we turn back at a village named Double Dragon do I realize that the Daning swarms with boats like ours, full of rubbernecking Chinese tourists.

"I'll tell you why," says Mrs. Shen. "China has just adopted a five-day work week. People who have the money now have enough time to take trips, and Chinese people do love sightseeing!"

The *Qiao Feng* makes it through the final of the Three Gorges that afternoon. Only four and a half miles long, Qutang Gorge is the most dramatic, the narrowest, the steepest and wildest of all. How can the immense volume of Yangtze water with its million tons of silt pass between these rock walls in a space merely 350 feet wide?

Buoys resembling toy boats topped by pyramids mark the passage. We idle to let a large, down-coming passenger ship whiz past. There is only room in the channel for one at a time, and it can't stop.

Here Isabella Bird watched, horrified, as a big junk swept past her and struck a rock. The junk flew into fragments as if it had exploded, with all hands lost. It had taken her ten days to get through the Three

Gorges, compared to our two days. The *Qiao Feng* rolls and shudders. Below deck, strange creaking, snapping noises sound like scurrying feet above the vibrating hum of the engine and the incessant, muffled bellowing of the ship's horn. They sound like ghosts.

Next day I meet ghosts galore when we dock at Fengdu, known as Ghost City. An ancient legend marks it as the spot

where the King of Hell summoned ghosts of the newly dead to be judged.

Historically, the Chinese seem always to have gone in heavily for ghosts. Yangtze junkmen refused to tie up at Fengdu for fear of ghosts sneaking on board, and dropped anchor offshore. Ships had enough trouble on the river with ghosts of drowned sailors hanging on behind them, ready to clamber up and make mischief.

Firecrackers and loud drums were the only sure way to scare them off.

Saturday mobs throng all 800 steps of Fengdu's mountain stairway. I stop frequently to catch my breath in temples filled with gaudy folk art, much of it restored and embellished in recent years. A marked stairstep shows that many of Fengdu's attractions will remain above the future water level, though thousands of people in

*Chicks and ducklings from nearby farms along the river fill baskets in Shibaozhai's weekly market.*

*A blue temple in Fengdu houses folkloric figures of demons and ghosts.*

the town below will be moved to a new site across the lake.

I envy sightseers riding a chairlift straight to the top. But the climb is worth it. Sculptured panoramas present a marvelously grotesque bureaucracy of ghostly functionaries skewering, roasting, and

*Chongqing's kids take ups and downs in stride.*

*Sparkling lights of Chongqing, commercial hub of western China, spread along the Yangtze.*

dismembering miscreants such as corrupt officials, disrespectful children, cheating shopkeepers, murderers, and gluttons. The crowds around me look happy, enjoying the outing, the moral lesson, and perhaps a secret frisson.

My last evening aboard the *Qiao Feng*

introduces me to Asia's craze of karaoke. The rage began in the 1980s in Japan, where *karaoke* means "empty orchestra," or "music looking for a singer."

A farewell party is announced. When we of the English table reach the fifth-floor karaoke parlor, the Taiwanese and Malaysian groups are already seated, talking excitedly, dressed to kill.

The huge TV screen is programmed to provide, along with moony landscapes and tableaux of sexy girls, the written words and the background music for, it seems, any song in the world.

Volunteers from the audience are expected to do the actual singing. The Malaysians are quickest to grab the microphone and toss off amazingly polished numbers with great brio. Slick performers in risqué costumes give me a jolt when I recognize them as the polite waiters and maids who have served us every day. My group is not allowed to escape. A menu of Western songs has been specially provided for us—with inadvertent typos. We pick "Love Me Fender" over "Three Loins in the Fountain" and sing sheepishly in unison while two of the Canadians do a 1950s jitterbug routine.

Farewells amid mountains of luggage. Chongqing fades into morning smog above us. From here the *Qiao Feng* will speed back to Wuhan, a whole day faster than its upstream voyage. Passengers head away from the Yangtze along well-worn tourist routes. I'm the only one hoping to follow the river farther.

Photographer George Steinmetz, jaunty in a baseball cap, meets me at a big American hotel. We are both eager to get out of Chongqing. Isabella Bird's "noble-looking, grey city" of half a million people is now a metropolis of more than 14 million that will soon dominate the end of the new lake. I can almost feel the pressure of all those human bodies.

George's map shows a long stretch— I guess 200 miles—of river between Chongqing and the next port, Luzhou. And it looks like another 100 miles to Yibin, the Yangtze's last—or first—navigable port. There will be no tourist facilities. Isabella wouldn't have minded, nor would I. But when I find that the small boat to Luzhou takes 36 hours battling upstream, it is lack of time, not comfort, that forces me ashore. By car, we can be in Luzhou in five hours.

Our driver, hired from a tourist company, turns up in a Toyota minivan. He is a city dude named Liu, dressed in a wide tie and a Western-style jacket, its left sleeve sporting a prominent, familiar blue-ribbon logo with the unlikely designer's name: PABST/ITALY. Liu strikes a karate pose and explains that the logo means "blue belt."

His girlfriend in black leather mini-shorts and platform shoes waves us off.

Liu is a terrible driver. Red Mao Zedong buttons festoon his rearview mirror to protect the car from accidents the way saints' medals dangle in the deadly taxis of other countries. We are well on our way before Liu admits that he has never driven beyond the city limits of Chongqing and does not have a map. From here on, George navigates.

None of my guidebooks mentions Luzhou—"an important trading city," according to Isabella. She noted its pretty location at the junction of the Tuo River and the Yangtze and its production of fine glazed-paper umbrellas. I, on the contrary, am struck by its strong, yeasty smell. And by its buses, the strangest I have ever seen. Each has on its roof rack a huge black gas balloon as big as the bus itself, which provides its fuel. Luzhou's modern industries are natural gas and sorghum-based liquor.

*Rice seedlings sprout in the rain near Zhuhai. Roughly 70 percent of China's rice grows in the Yangtze basin.*

*Waterfall douses tourists and pilgrims on path to centuries-old caves of Buddhist monks in the cliffs of Zhuhai.*

A sea of multicolored umbrellas turns the Yangtze's grassy sand flats into a vast picnic playground while the water is low. Luzhou, without any tourists, seems to be enjoying itself.

The road to Yibin hugs the south bank of the wide, racing river. Steady drizzle turns a long unpaved stretch into red mud. I decide to give Liu a break and take a detour. I have heard that not far from here—in a protected natural area called Zhuhai, the Bamboo Sea—there are Ming dynasty Buddhist caves. A slightly better road leads to a high spot overlooking a thousand acres of unbroken, pale green bamboo. The wind picks up, and rippling waves chase each other across undulating hillsides. The forest truly looks like water.

I sleep well at a newly refurbished rest house. George and I are up at dawn. We want to see the caves in tranquillity, as they must once have been. We follow a swift stream through silent groves of bamboo 50 feet high to a waterfall that plunges over an immense cliff. Way, way below us, the Yu River winds through an intricate mosaic of rice terraces. Buddhist monks could hardly have found a better place to contemplate eternity. Our path leads us precariously over the cliff's edge.

Just below the rim, in a little stone booth, sits a wide-awake ticket seller. Beyond the foaming waterfall, a huge reclining Buddha has been carved into the rock face—dated 1993. The old caves, brightly restored and expanded, are dwarfed by a giant new statue of Guanyin, the Goddess of Mercy, trickling water from an outsize urn. "All done with donations from Overseas Chinese!" says the manager of the attached teahouse happily. When I clamber up to the bamboo forest again, souvenir stands line the path.

I think of Isabella as we head back toward the Yangtze. She would feel at home following the small Yu River. Wooden rivercraft—sampans with hooped matting for shelter and big, sturdy *wupans*—ply the river with sweeping oars. Brightly colored family laundry hangs out to dry on a flat-bottomed houseboat much like hers. A raft of bamboo floats by with a makeshift mast and sail. While the Yangtze changes and develops, the age-old river life continues serenely along its tributaries.

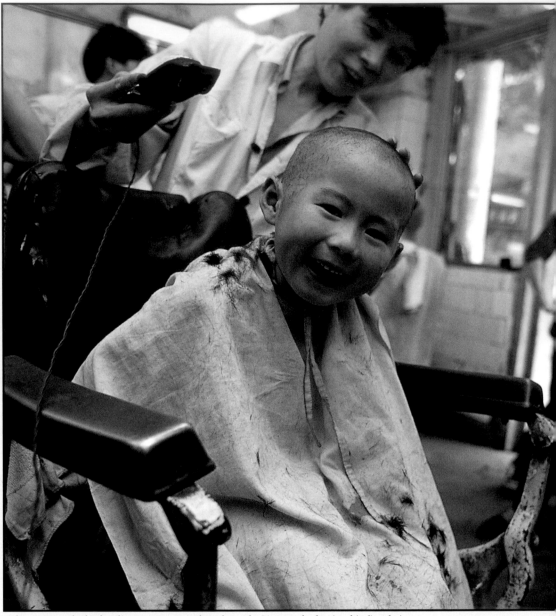

*A boy gets ready for broiling summer weather along the Yangtze by having his first haircut.*

We rejoin the Yangtze near Yibin. Two pagodas, one black, one white, look down from opposite hilltops on the meeting of two rivers—the tan-colored, silt-laden Golden Sand and the wide, murky green Min. Here at the starting point of the Long River, two distinctive waters flow side by side, refusing to mingle for as far as my eye can see. The city, on a high point between the rivers, appears to embrace them both with its outstretched bridges.

The outskirts of Yibin are not picturesque. On the green-water side of the Yangtze, a pulp mill spews black smoke into the air and globs of pollution into the river. The muddy-water side has a sprawling shipyard. I glimpse a new cruise ship in a spidery cage of bamboo scaffolding on the riverbank. Resplendent in an undercoat of orange paint, she is as big as the *Qiao Feng*. During the summer the Yangtze will give her a natural launching when it rises and floats her free.

Beyond the bridge over the Golden Sand, Yibin snoozes—an unhurried city with flower gardens on balconies and roofs. Bright yellow pedicabs are as common as cars. In the middle of the street by

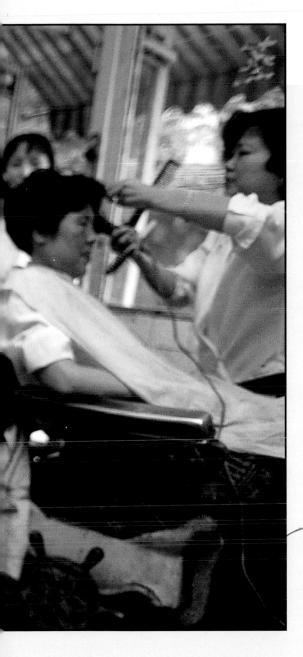

we say we're the *first* one. Because we are." And he proceeds to tell me about the great day in 1986 when that mattered.

A Chinese rafting team, the first ever to raft the whole length of the Yangtze River from its source to Shanghai, arrived, exhausted and triumphant, at Yibin. After 2,000 miles of terror on the Golden Sand, after watching competing teams come to grief, they had reached the first port on the Yangtze—and knew they were safe.

"We lined the shores and bridges with balloons and banners and flags. Oh, you should have seen it!" Wei crowed. "They rested for two full days in Yibin."

Wei offers me a drink. Yibin's five-grain liquor is famous throughout China, he says. The best there is. He's been tippling it for more than 60 years and should know. I'm almost ashamed to decline. But I leave him and go hunting for George. He's in a teahouse, watching beady-eyed old men and women play mah-jongg.

oreigners are rare in Yibin. We are met with blank, unabashed stares. It's a pleasant surprise when a well-dressed man in his thirties makes friends with us on the street and begs us to come eat at his five-table Seahorse Sidewalk Restaurant. "I'll cook anything you like, anything at all!" He is as good as his word.

Xiang Yanping, like many urban Chinese, is moonlighting. By day he is an army officer but his heart is clearly in his cheerful, successful restaurant. His attractive wife, an accountant in the municipal government, runs the Seahorse Karaoke Parlor next door.

I find myself wondering when they sleep. But I'm reluctant to inquire, so instead, I ask, "Why the name Seahorse?"

Xiang delightfully brings out a bottle of

our hotel, a little boy tries out a bicycle with training wheels, with his mother strolling unconcerned beside him. We say goodbye to Liu, who can hardly wait to get back to Chongqing.

A brand new Port Authority building stands empty, overlooking the docks where the green and brown waters meet. One dock is a floating karaoke bar. An elderly caretaker, Wei Laobao, ambles over to chat, clanking a great string of keys. He's slightly drunk and wants to be sure I appreciate Yibin. "We're the 13th port city on the Yangtze, the last one," he announces. "But

*Thousand-year-old Dafo, world's largest sitting Buddha statue, surveys the Min River near Leshan.*

the medicinal "tonic" that helps make his restaurant popular. It is the famous Yibin five-grain liquor with a little pickled seahorse in the bottle. He picks it out with his chopsticks and pours us each a glass for our health.

Late in the evening their eight-year-old son shows up at the restaurant, smartly dressed in a suit. He has been at his after-school tutoring session. He shakes my hand, pipes "Hello, Auntie" in English, then politely kisses me. He is already on the road to success.

In a park with pretty gardens and pavilions, I come upon a wild, hidden grotto. Under an overhanging crag entwined with banyan roots, a brook was diverted, many centuries ago, into an elegant, man-made meandering channel. Free-spirited poets, escaped or banished from the imperial court, once gathered here to float their wine cups down the winding stream and write. Their poems are engraved on the flat face of the rock, some in fine calligraphy, some in slapdash style. Yibin sheltered and inspired them.

I am at the end of my journey. I have seen the beginning of the Long River from its first port. I have followed fearless, curious Isabella Bird as far as I can go. And I have touched Mrs. Shen's "real China."

There is one last thing I hope to do before heading home. At Leshan, up the Min River, a half-day's drive from Yibin, sits Dafo, the 231-foot-high carved statue of a sitting Buddha. Cut into a cliff in another millennium to protect boatmen, his size and unyielding presence seem to sum up the Yangtze River itself.

I sit on Dafo's toenail beside the turbulent Min and ponder. The world's largest dam will bring huge change to this land of more than a billion people. I picture China gazing simultaneously backward to its ancient, colorful history on a wave of Asian tourists, and forward to an unimaginable future with the Seahorse family and Liu. But for me the present moment suffices.

*Winding steps carved in rock form a precipitous pilgrim path between Dafo's toes and head.*

# Traveling
# Canada's
# Transcontinental
# Railroad

by Thurston Clarke

Photographs by Maggie Steber

*Moraine Lake attracts tourists to Banff National Park, created in 1885 as a spin-off of the transcontinental railway.*

*Leaving Jasper National Park, the* Canadian *passes through boundless peaks and forests to reach Vancouver.*

anadians are a great people for superlatives, fond of boasting about having the longest coastline, highest tides, and biggest bay, and, after Russia, of being the largest country on earth. After traveling almost 4,000 miles across this country, and after dangling one foot in the Atlantic at Halifax and, two weeks and two changes of train later, the other in the Pacific at Vancouver, I am ready to argue for a new superlative. If you believe, as I do, that there is something inherently exotic about sheer size, then a journey by train across Canada makes it seem like one of the most exotic nations in the world.

I have never prayed for a safe journey before boarding a train, but this trip was so long I made an exception and stopped at St. Paul's Anglican Church in Halifax, the oldest Protestant church in Canada. Parishioners fill the Massachusetts-style box pews to worship over the burial vaults of homesick loyalists who fought to keep Massachusetts British.

The British North America Act of 1867 created a Canada composed of Quebec, Ontario, New Brunswick, and Nova Scotia. The last two joined only after the government promised to build a railway connecting them to the west. British Columbia signed on four years later, when Prime Minister John A. MacDonald pledged a transcontinental line linking east and west. His parliamentary opposition denounced

it as "an act of insane recklessness," but between 1881 and 1885 the Canadian Pacific Railway laid tracks across the nation, thereby opening Canada's west to millions of European immigrants, who eventually settled the provinces of Manitoba, Alberta, and Saskatchewan.

Canadian historian Pierre Berton considers this the defining moment in his nation's history. He wrote, "We have no blood in our history—no searing civil war, no surgical revolution. We are the only nation in the world created non-violently by the building of a railway."

However, a violent moment occurred in Halifax on the morning of December 6, 1917. One of the most lethal and powerful man-made explosions prior to Hiroshima devastated the Halifax waterfront. Triggered by the collision of a munitions ship with another vessel, the explosion left almost 2,000 people dead and destroyed the station from which many immigrant pioneers had headed west. Because of this tragedy, the overnight *Ocean* to Montreal now leaves from a sturdier limestone building away from the busiest part of the harbor.

I arrived an hour before departure to find my fellow passengers gathering under the station's girders and skylight, eyeing one another like freshmen on the first day of classes. Like many others I saw in Canada, the Halifax station had been lovingly restored; its wood paneling shone, and its brass fixtures gleamed. As the conductor

CANADIAN PACIFIC LIMITED

*British royalty travels by Canadian rail in 1951.*

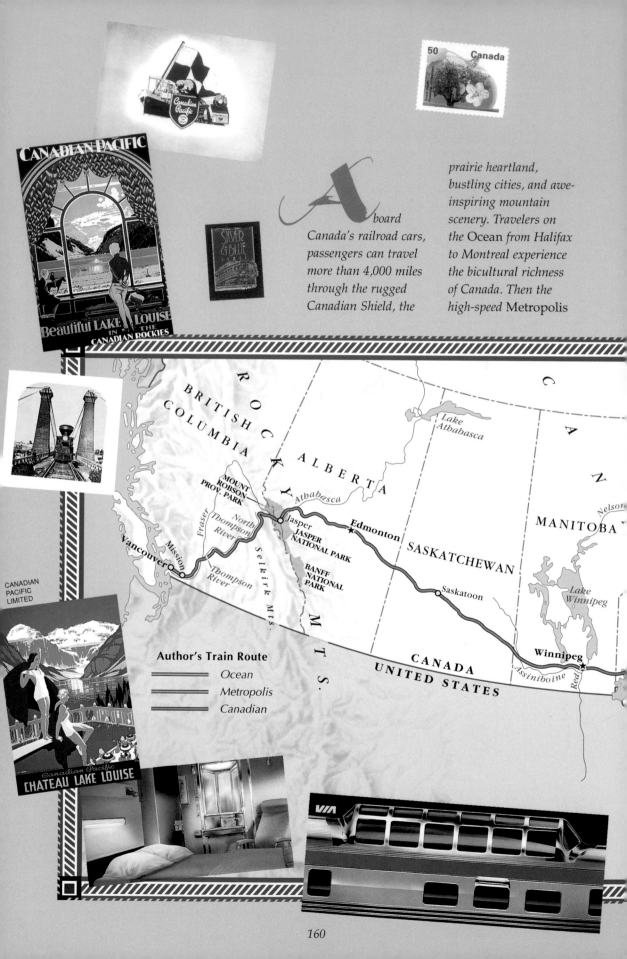

50 Canada

CANADIAN PACIFIC

Beautiful LAKE LOUISE
IN THE
CANADIAN ROCKIES

**A**board Canada's railroad cars, passengers can travel more than 4,000 miles through the rugged Canadian Shield, the prairie heartland, bustling cities, and awe-inspiring mountain scenery. Travelers on the *Ocean* from Halifax to Montreal experience the bicultural richness of Canada. Then the high-speed *Metropolis*

CANADIAN
PACIFIC
LIMITED

*Canadian Pacific*
CHATEAU LAKE LOUISE

**Author's Train Route**
Ocean
Metropolis
Canadian

R O C K Y

BRITISH COLUMBIA

A L B E R T A

SASKATCHEWAN

C A N

MANITOBA

Lake Athabasca

Athabasca

Nelson

MOUNT ROBSON PROV. PARK

Jasper

JASPER NATIONAL PARK

BANFF NATIONAL PARK

Edmonton

Fraser

North Thompson River

Thompson River

Mission

Vancouver

S e l k i r k   M t s.

M T S.

Saskatoon

Lake Winnipeg

Winnipeg

C A N A D A
UNITED STATES

Assiniboine

Red

VIA

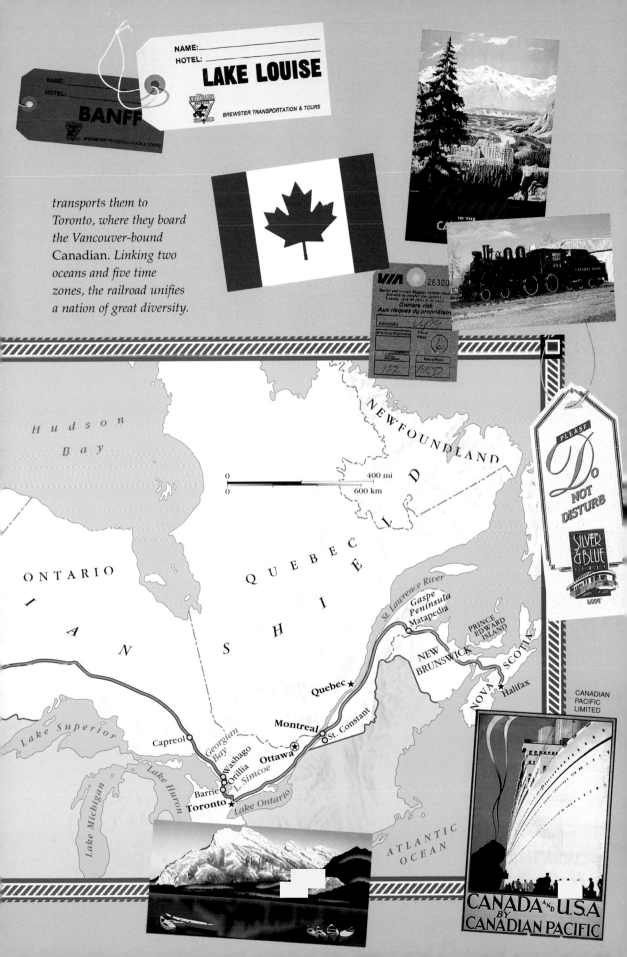

NAME:
HOTEL:

**LAKE LOUISE**

BREWSTER TRANSPORTATION & TOURS

NAME:
HOTEL:

**BANFF**

BREWSTER TRANSPORTATION & TOURS

*transports them to Toronto, where they board the Vancouver-bound Canadian. Linking two oceans and five time zones, the railroad unifies a nation of great diversity.*

VIA 26300
Station and on-train baggage transfer check
Étiquette de transfert des bagages à station, dans les gares et les trains
Owners risk
Aux risques du propriétaire

PLEASE **D**O NOT DISTURB

SILVER & BLUE

VIA

CANADIAN PACIFIC LIMITED

H u d s o n
B a y

NEWFOUNDLAND

0        400 mi
0        600 km

ONTARIO

QUEBEC

C A N A D I A N   S H I E L D

St. Lawrence River

Gaspe Peninsula
Matapedia

PRINCE EDWARD ISLAND

NEW BRUNSWICK

NOVA SCOTIA
★ Halifax

Quebec ★

Lake Superior

Capreol ○

Georgian Bay

Washago
Orillia
L. Simcoe

Barrie

**Toronto** ★

Lake Huron

Lake Michigan

Montreal

Ottawa ★

St. Constant ○

Lake Ontario

ATLANTIC OCEAN

CANADA ᴬᴺᴰ U.S.A
BY CANADIAN PACIFIC

*Kilted students reenact military duties of the 78th Highlanders at the Halifax Citadel National Historic Site.*

opened the gates, we rushed to the gleaming stainless-steel train. The 12 streamlined 1955 Budd cars seemed both futuristic and dated, as if a time machine had brought them to this gritty, redbrick and clapboard city from either the future or the past. The *Ocean* promised a measure of speed, with comfort and safety, and reflected loving maintenance.

I had planned to unpack fast and rush to the domed Park Car at the rear of the train. Instead, I was mesmerized by how everything fit into the coat closet-size roomette. There was nothing digital, nothing operated by a keyboard, remote control, or computer chip. Yet within easy reach were knobs to regulate fresh air and temperature, a toilet hidden beneath the footstool, and a leather pouch over the bed for eyeglasses and watch. There was even a metal box for

*Halifax's Old Town Clock has kept time since 1803.*

shoes, with doors opening on two sides, which used to allow a porter to shine and replace the shoes without disturbing the passenger.

My chair folded over so a bed could slide out or be pulled from the wall. My sink pulled down from another wall. When pushed back in place, it automatically dumped its wastewater onto the tracks. I tested it and remembered tipping up a similar sink in our bedroom on the *Twentieth Century Limited* during a 1955 journey from New York to Chicago, thereby spilling my mother's nylons beside an Ohio cornfield. Then I also remembered being stuck on the *Orient Express* in 1967, when lightning exploded charges placed by the suspicious Turks and Greeks at either side of a bridge connecting their nations. I recalled passengers unrolling carpets on the corridor floor of an antique Dakar-to-Bamako sleeping car train in Mali and bowing to Mecca as we rocked past giant anthills. I realized that every overnight train ride evokes the ghosts of earlier journeys and yields experiences to compare with future ones.

When the *Ocean* departed with the characteristic railway jerk, instead of asking myself, "How soon will I get there?" —as I do whenever a plane accelerates—I wondered, "Whom will I meet, what will I see, and what will happen before I stick my foot in the Pacific?" Then I did a Charlie Chaplin-style walk through swaying corridors to the Park Car.

It was empty except for a honeymooning German couple with their noses in the same Baedeker I was using. Unlike the long-distance *Canadian*, which I would soon take west from Toronto, this was a homey train for local people who joined it at small stations along the line.

Most of the passengers were young people escaping the Maritime Provinces' hardscrabble economy, families with children rubbing sleepy eyes the moment they boarded, and students who drank coffee and stared bug-eyed at underlined textbooks, ignoring like seasoned commuters what was flashing by the windows.

We appeared to be the main event as we rolled through the black forests and rolling farms of Nova Scotia and New Brunswick—the only passenger train of the day to Montreal, Canada's second largest metropolitan area. As we snaked around the back side of Halifax, train-spotting fathers and sons on bridges followed us with binoculars. Two boys stopped roughhousing on a float in the middle of a round lake to stare at us openmouthed. In a lumberyard the size of a stadium parking lot, a workman braked his forklift and waved his cap. Children jumped off swings under

*European tourist gazes through dining car window as the* Ocean *crosses New Brunswick's Miramichi River.*

*Schoolchildren parade past a massive locomotive in the Canadian Railway Museum in St. Constant.*

*International Fireworks Competition produces a dazzling display over Montreal's Jacques Cartier Bridge.*

Bonjour! *Calèche driver waves in Old Montreal.*

a tree large enough to decorate New York's Rockefeller Center at Christmas and dashed toward us shouting joyfully. As we crossed the vast Tantramar Marshes—once called the largest hayfield in the world, and now home to an abundance of waterfowl—hands shot from car windows. Whole families waved in unison.

Had I stayed in my compartment with its single window on the right-hand side of the train, I would have missed half these sights. Instead, I spent most of my time in the Park Car, upstairs in its dome or downstairs in its bullet-shaped lounge. I liked the way the lounge armchairs faced one another and encouraged conversation. I also liked the six wall clocks reminding you that Canada sprawls across two more time zones than the United States.

I admired how every streamlined detail of the interior had been restored, even down to the fluorescent light in the handrail leading upstairs to the dome. But most of all I gravitated to this car because it supplied that unique railway sensation of traveling fast through other people's lives, of watching track disappear through a curved rear window while you speed on to the next great city or natural wonder.

I stayed awake for the Quebec border and disembarked at Matapedia to watch us pick up the sleepers and coaches of the *Chaleur*, the triweekly train from the Gaspe Peninsula. A crusty porter named Donnie

Uhren said most porters were at least 25-year veterans. VIA Rail Canada, the national passenger train service, has been shrinking its routes. So many Maritime Provinces trains have been discontinued that only the most senior employees remain.

Supervising sleeping car service is not the kind of job you might imagine to be full of surprises, but the service manager, Gordon MacDonald, told me he has stayed on the job for 31 years because it is never monotonous. He insisted that every departure sets his adrenaline flowing. Every group of passengers is different, so every run is a unique adventure. Consider, for example, the belongings left behind. Gordon has found a cupboard stuffed with fur coats, and even an artificial leg!

I had seen the sun set behind a lonely forest in New Brunswick, where people speak English. I raised my shade at 5 a.m.

*Local step-dance troupe enlivens Montreal's Old Port.*

to see signs in French and a freighter gliding down the St. Lawrence. Across the river, the fortifications of Quebec glowed yellow in the summer sunrise. Towering above them were the turrets of the Château Frontenac, the most distinctive of the Canadian Pacific's railway-chateau hotels. It serves as a reminder that Canada can thank its railroad for some of its architectural monuments as well as for its unity.

Few views can communicate so much history at a glance. Framed in my window were the Citadelle, a star-shaped fort that forms the eastern flank of the fortifications of Quebec, and the cliffs that General Wolfe's redcoats had scaled in 1759 at the Battle of Quebec. Beyond them lay the Plains of Abraham, where Wolfe suffered a mortal wound but the British troops went on to defeat Montcalm's French. This victory, with the ensuing Treaty of Paris, signed in 1763, guaranteed that the Quebecois would be the French-speaking minority in an English colony.

*T*he differences between the province of Quebec and the Maritime Provinces seemed greater than those between many European countries. I had traded gabled, clapboard houses for brick, stucco, and aluminum ones, matchstick Protestant churches for granite Catholic ones, and lumberjacks for old men carrying baguettes in bicycle panniers. The change was so dramatic that by the time we swung across the St. Lawrence into Montreal I almost expected to see officious *douaniers* demanding to inspect our bags before admitting us to the second largest French-speaking city in the world.

Montreal is Canada's great railway town, site of the 19th-century scheming that produced that country's first transcon-

tinental track, and later the headquarters for the Canadian Pacific Railway (CPR), Canadian National (CN), and VIA lines. During an eight-hour layover, I tried to preserve the illusion that trains are still the city's principal enterprise by visiting CPR's Windsor Station. But although its romantic turrets and castle-like facade signified power and wealth, the station's recent abandonment by even commuter trains was a more accurate indication of the true state of North American rail travel.

*"Monument to Multiculturalism," in front of Toronto's Union Station, celebrates the city's diverse population.*

That same day I had lunch at the venerable Beaver Club in the Queen Elizabeth Hotel, which is connected by tunnel to Montreal's long-distance passenger station, the Gare Centrale. My companions were VIA executives Malcolm Andrews and Paul Raynor, the modern descendants of railroad barons such as William Van Horne and Thomas Shaughnessy, if not in achievements then certainly in enthusiasm.

Andrews has a good railway pedigree. His uncle was a conductor and his aunt a station mistress in his native Nova Scotia. Andrews started with the railway two decades ago as a teenager, working as a sleeping car porter during his summer vacations. He and Raynor agree that one reason they love traveling on overnight passenger trains is the secure, "cocoon-like" feeling you have while riding on them, which is missing in a car or a plane.

They appeared as determined to preserve what Raynor called "a viable passenger network" as Van Horne had been to build it. I heard an echo of his enthusiasm in their boast that VIA's dome cars have become a national totem on a par with the Mountie. They bragged that the *Metropolis* intercity express I would be catching in a few hours was the longest nonstop passenger run in the world—a 3-hour-41-minute, 323-mile trip from suburban Dorval to Toronto, which, with minor adjustments, could be reduced another 20 minutes.

The best I can say for this train is that it was fast. It came with all the customary tortures of air travel: cramped seats, reheated tray meals, rolling beverage cart, and narrow aisles. Unlike the *Ocean*'s heavy Budd cars, its relatively newer coaches rattled and bumped. Because there was no bar or lounge car, I met only the businessman next to me, who slumbered and snored. With nowhere to go except the toilet, I passed the time as I would on a plane— reading or sleeping.

Our arrival in Toronto made up for everything. A flaming sun was sliding behind a wall of skyscrapers as we pulled

*Etched glass panel features a sandpiper.*

into one of North America's legendary stations. Like Grand Central in New York, Union Station is a glorious temple of travel, boasting an arched tile ceiling, limestone columns stretching a city block, a 250-square-foot Great Hall that is the largest room in Canada, and those hallmarks of every great urban terminal—echoing footsteps and dust motes dancing in light shafts. Carved beneath the cornice were the names of the Canadian cities owing their growth and prosperity to the tracks below.

I wheeled my bag from the station to

*The refurbished interior of the dining car recreates the art deco style of the* Canadian *in the 1950s.*

the landmark Royal York Hotel through a short tunnel that had been the first underground pedestrian walkway in a city now crisscrossed by them. The Royal York is a skyscraper version of the traditional Canadian Pacific chateau hotel. Capped by the same trademark green copper roof as the Château Frontenac, it was built to the standards of a grand European hotel so that foreign dignitaries and royalty arriving in Toronto by train could instantly feel at home. It is no longer the tallest building in the British Empire—as it was when completed in 1928—but its 1,535 rooms still make it one of the largest hotels in the world. It sparkles like fine jewelry among the Gotham City-like skyscrapers that have since claimed Toronto's skyline.

When I emerged from the tunnel into the hotel lobby, the throngs of shoppers, travelers, and conventioneers meeting, hugging, and slapping backs under the glorious two-story, hand-painted Italian Renaissance ceiling told me I was in the much loved gathering place of a major city.

Just before leaving Toronto I had coffee

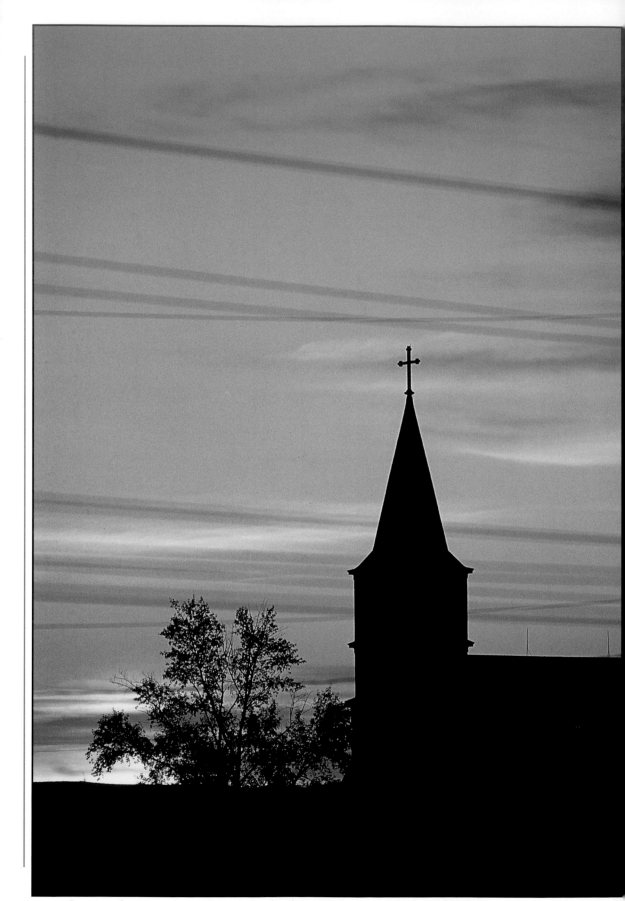

*Sunset reaches across the prairie to a quiet church near the border of Ontario and Manitoba.*

in the Union Station café with John Teplicky, a diesel-size, silver-haired man who is the most senior passenger train engineer in Canada. With the nonchalance of a veteran transatlantic pilot, he described level-crossing collisions—the most memorable of which involved a stalled brick truck—making it sound as if riding the *Canadian* to Vancouver was still a reckless adventure. But when I asked if he had ever struck anyone, his ice blue eyes filled with tears as he recounted hitting a ten-year-old boy who had been running across a bridge as the train rounded a bend. "It goes with the job," he said, as much to himself as to me. "Very few engineers haven't had an experience like it."

*Couple from Texas savors the passing scenery.*

When the *Canadian* pulled out of Toronto for Vancouver the next day, many of my fellow passengers were burly, retired British train engineers on holiday. As we left the station they broke into applause and cheers, then stormed the bar and turned their backs to the windows. The only things they missed at first were warehouses, housing tracts corralled behind fences, and Lake Simcoe, where Jet Skis buzzed like millpond insects.

In the lake town of Barrie we passed a go-cart rally, with hundreds of spectators in identical "Grand Prix of Barrie" T-shirts. In a field outside Orillia a teenage couple making out on a blanket jumped up as if surprised by their parents. Outside

Washago a woman in a bikini landed a fish and the man sharing the rowboat hugged her, almost tipping them over.

Then about a hundred miles from Toronto, almost as if in the snap of a finger, the people, towns, farms, and roads vanished as we plunged into one of the most forbidding wildernesses in North America—the great Canadian Shield. The abruptness of the change was unsettling. The sunlit and idyllic scenes of a few miles back lay in the shadow of a wasteland of scrappy forest, dripping ferns, skeleton armies of white birches, midnight black bogs, and granite-fringed lakes with water so clear that looking at them made me thirsty.

When the *Canadian* traverses the Rockies, it usually shares a pass or valley with at least one twisty highway. But here in Ontario, the ground is part of a vast blanket of rock left by the retreating glaciers of several ice ages. We saw neither roads nor towns, and with the exception of an occasional fisherman's cabin, the landscape has remained the same since laborers laid the first tracks.

It was this terrain, rather than the Rockies or the corkscrew turns of British Columbia's valleys, that had presented Canada's railway pioneers with their greatest obstacles. The boulders, bogs, and sparkling lakes were a great terrain for anyone looking to catch fish, hunt game, or canoe forever, but hell on men blasting through slabs of granite, pouring fill into swamps, and bridging hundreds of rivers. The terrain had prompted Van Horne to bemoan its hundreds of miles of "engineering impossibilities."

The insistent way Ontario repeated itself, endlessly stammering, "lake, rock, woods...lake, rock, woods," finally silenced even the jocular British train drivers. Soon everyone was scanning the forests and lakes looking for, well, looking for anything! I saw three moose standing up to their knees in a marsh, a woman spotted a bear, and soon everyone was acting like hunters on safari. Then it grew dark, and the windows threw our reflections back at us.

When passengers praised the *Canadian*'s luxury, they usually meant the linen tablecloths and comfortable berths. For me, the greatest luxury was seeing this

*Supplies for the kitchen sail aboard in Winnipeg.*

rugged country without spending days paddling a canoe or nights under mosquito netting. I was dining on grilled salmon while bridging fast-moving, rock-strewn rivers capable of eviscerating any canoe.

During a 15-minute stop in Capreol we took on water and an exotic cargo of canoes, fishing rods, and coolers of fresh food for camps accessible only by train. We were already an hour late, and a conductor predicted we would lose another four hours before reaching Winnipeg tomorrow afternoon. The culprit was a record heat wave, which threatened to bend the rails and create "sun kinks," which can cause derailments. It forced us to reduce our speed to 45 mph. Service manager Ron Derksen told me this was a small price to pay to avoid a derailment. Once a derailment in the Rockies blocked the *Canadian* in the front while an avalanche blocked the rear. His passengers were marooned two days, but were supplied by helicopter.

The fact that a train has tracks to jump, and that its route has seen the passage of a century of other passenger cars and freights, gives a rail journey a historical backdrop that even the longest trip by air can never match. I liked knowing that at various points I was using the same tracks as the 7.5 billion dollars in gold reserves that the Bank of England had dispatched to

*Booming Winnipeg blends traditional and modern.*

*Open-air café brings a new look to Forks Market, formerly a rail depot, behind Winnipeg's Union Station.*

*Panoramic views from the Canadian's domed observation cars entice tourists to travel by train.*

*Well-placed mirrors maximize space in a compact bedroom.*

Canadian vaults during the darkest days of World War II. Over these tracks the fabled early-20th-century "silk trains" used to rush the multimillion-dollar cargoes of perishable raw silk from west-coast Canadian ports to east-coast U.S. buyers. The silk trains set speed records and, at remote junctions such as Capreol, attracted sightseers who pressed themselves against station walls, fearing that the vacuum created by these rocketing expresses might suck them under the wheels.

The next afternoon we left the Canadian Shield as abruptly as we had entered it. I looked up from a magazine to see barns, silos, and grain, then a pickup racing us down a parallel road. I saw small towns founded by late 19th-century squatters who had guessed where these tracks would be laid. After 24 hours of rocks, lakes, and trees, any human mark on the landscape was strangely comforting. People pointed out children on a swing set ("Look...children!") and a school bus ("Hey, did you catch that yellow bus?") as if they were as strange and wonderful as yesterday's beaver dams and moose. But even before I could become accustomed to the monster farms and grain elevators, the skyscrapers of Winnipeg appeared, soaring from the prairie like the Emerald City in the *The Wizard of Oz*.

Winnipeg had once been the most important riverine junction of the

*Chef flips pancakes in the train's kitchen while his assistant scrambles eggs for hungry passengers' brunch.*

*Private bedroom offers a passenger space to stretch out and enjoy fast-changing landscapes.*

Canadian west. For centuries Indians had met at this confluence of the Assiniboine and Red Rivers for trade and ceremonial rites. In 1738 European trappers named this site The Forks, where they built Fort Rouge, their first trading post.

When the CPR chose Winnipeg as its main supply depot in 1881, the city was suddenly flooded with timber, rails, spikes, and 3,000 laborers, on its way to becoming the most important rail junction of the Canadian prairie. The ensuing land boom attracted 300 real estate speculators and doubled its population of 16,000 in only a year. When the Louisa Railway Bridge opened, the *Winnipeg Free Press* described the accompanying celebration as "a great, hilarious, illimitable guzzle" of free beer and champagne, and a "debauch…the largest and most varied the city has seen for many a day."

Immediately after crossing the Red River, my train

*CPR emblem from the 1940s.*

stopped at the elevated platform of Winnipeg's Union Station. It offered a fine view of The Forks, where a collection of historic warehouses, stables, and a freight terminal had recently been turned into a lively complex of restaurants, stores, and cafés, making it again the city's symbolic meeting place.

I checked my bag and walked through the waiting room's soaring beaux arts rotunda, over a crack in its marble floor left by the thousands of World War II regiments who made the mistake of marching across it without breaking ranks, and out a back door to The Forks. When the *Canadian* rumbled over the trestle bridge on its way to Jasper, I was already drinking iced tea in a café overlooking a dock where pleasure boats had replaced long canoes unloading pelts.

Even at dusk the heat was scorching. A wind as dry and crackly as any desert sirocco rattled awnings and caused

roller skaters to flick their eyes to the horizon, searching for tornadoes. The following evening a ferocious storm swept through town, toppling trees and power lines, peeling roofs, and catching me strolling along the Red River. It was the dusty, furnace-hot wind, menacing yellow light, and towering black clouds that only get cooked up in the center of a vast continent—in Africa's Sahara, The Steppes of Asia, or the vast North American prairies.

The next day I continued west through Saskatchewan, where the horizon was broken only by blinking radio towers, skyscraper-like grain elevators, and the silvery onion domes of Orthodox churches built by Ukrainian immigrants. The land was so flat you could imagine a puff of wind triggering a chain reaction that would send grain waving all the way to the American border. In this sea of wheat the farms resembled islands—just circles of trees and high shrubbery surrounding outbuildings and clapboard farmhouses. On each farm I imagined a boy hearing our whistle and planning his escape to the city.

Van Horne had been a stickler for passenger comfort. When transcontinental service began in 1885, his advertisement promised, "…there will be no hardships to endure, no difficulties to overcome, and no dangers and annoyances. You shall see mighty rivers, vast forests, boundless plains, stupendous mountains, and wonders unimaginable; and you shall see all in comfort, nay in luxury." Nowhere was this promise more quickly or unarguably delivered than in the company's dining cars. Within a year of construction feats that saw CPR's workers menaced by grizzlies, blizzards, and rockslides, passengers were enjoying the sumptuous comforts of

*The original Canadian Pacific rail line snakes through the snowcapped Rocky Mountains in Banff National Park.*

*Spirelike spruces edge the shore of Cavell Lake near a snowfield in Jasper National Park.*

tooled-leather berths, fine silver, and what one advertisement touted as cooking with "a wide reputation for excellence."

Railway cars in Europe and the U.S. were already famous for their luxury and food. But only in Canada was the transition so fast from construction to late-Victorian elegance, or the contrast so great between the white-glove presentation of Fraser River salmon and antelope steak in the dining car and the wild country just outside the window where they had been bagged.

The four dinners I sampled between Halifax and Vancouver were as good as those in any first-class hotel. In its glory days before 1970, VIA even offered pastries baked on board and fluffy omelets served on silver platters.

The atmosphere in the dining car also provided a link with the early days. You still heard the wind-chime tinkle of china

and silver as you rounded a curve, and still enjoyed the feeling of accomplishing two things at once that came with eating a fine dinner while rolling toward the Pacific. Food still came from a lilliputian kitchen where pots could never be overfilled, knives had to be carefully wielded, and meat slicers and fryers were prohibited.

The two-across seating and two-hour dinners forced you to meet fellow passengers. Our conversations were interrupted by pauses to admire the scenery and were memorably serene, as if the gentle rocking had slowed everyone's metabolism.

The dinner I enjoyed most occurred a few hours out of Winnipeg. The steward seated me across from Mike and Beverly Bayly, a handsome ranching couple from central California, who provided more proof for my theory that train buffs are the self-proclaimed aristocrats of travel. For them, the journey was more important than the destination, and their idea of a perfect vacation was to ride a train.

While distant car headlights swept wheat fields like spotlights and a cloudless sky offered a planetarium view of the heavens, Mike described railway journeys to Machu Picchu in Peru, across Scandinavia, and from Perth to Adelaide, Australia. When I asked which had been his favorite, he laughed. "Comparing them is like comparing beautiful women!"

I asked the Baylys why they loved trains, and they mentioned the relaxing clickety-clack of the wheels, the nighttime whistle, changing scenery, serendipitous meetings with passengers, and the fact that it was a real vacation because no one could bother you. Finally they just smiled and shook their heads, unable to explain any further an affection they obviously considered as natural as breathing.

The next morning the ground began to ripple and roll as if someone were pulling it like a rug. In Alberta, cattle and sheep replaced silos and soybeans, men rode horses instead of tractors, fences separated pastures, red barns vanished, trees thickened, and ridges gave way to foothills.

We joined the Athabasca River and followed its valley up into Jasper National Park, the largest of Canada's four contiguous Rocky Mountain preserves. I luxuriated in the views of luminous glaciers, ramparts of snowcapped mountains, gushing waterfalls, and elk grazing across a wide, watery valley. They seemed all the more wonderful because I was not contending with the speeding logging trucks and sweaty palms that come with mountain driving. Instead, I was relaxing in one of the *Canadian*'s dome cars.

These peaks reminded me of the Swiss Alps, perhaps because I usually see them by train. I am *(Continued on page 188)*

*Impressive antlers proclaim a bull elk's dominant status as he shepherds his harem across the Athabasca River.*

# William Van Horne

*William Van Horne, revered chairman of the Canadian Pacific Railway, poses around 1905.*

**W**illiam Van Horne was to railway men what Paul Bunyan was to lumberjacks, except that the larger-than-life Van Horne actually lived, and his prodigious feats of railway construction really happened. He was born in an Illinois log cabin in 1843, raised in poverty, and began his railway career as a telegraph messenger.

By the age of 28 Van Horne had become the youngest railway superintendent in the world. Within ten years he was general manager of the Chicago, Milwaukee & St. Paul Railway. He was already famous for his inexhaustible energy, practical knowledge of every aspect of railroading, and eccentric range of pastimes.

Van Horne could drive a locomotive, lay track, and work out complicated timetables in his head. A skillful amateur architect and draftsman, he sometimes designed the stations himself. He collected porcelain and fossils and was a noted gardener and gourmand.

One surveyor remembered seeing him smoking one of his trademark foot-long cigars while, at the same time, holding forth on an intricate engineering subject and executing a "splendid etching" on the blotting pad in front of him. A fellow American railroader called him "the ablest railroad executive in the world" and compared him with Ulysses S. Grant. Van Horne's stocky build, large head, beard, gruff manner, and ruthless determination also gave him a certain resemblance to the famous general.

In 1881 James J. Hill, executive committee member of the Canadian Pacific Railway, persuaded Van Horne to become the general manager and to supervise construction of Canada's transcontinental railway. He began his tenure in 1882 by brashly promising to lay 500 miles of rail across the Canadian prairies before the end of the year.

To achieve this unheard-of feat, he established mobile material yards on flatcars that could be moved quickly to new locations. At the end of the line he employed unusual three-story cars consisting of offices and dining rooms on the bottom level and workers' dormitories on the top two. They traveled westward as the track was laid each day. According to one observer, construction appeared to keep pace with the oxcarts of the settlers following them.

Despite the worst flood in years, his crews completed 418 miles of main and 110 miles of branch line by the end of 1882. By the time the ceremonial last spike was driven into a stretch of track at Craigellachie, British Columbia, in 1885, Van Horne had literally laid some of the rails himself, becoming a figure of near-mythical strength and determination.

According to one tale, when the half-completed Stoney Creek Bridge was threatened by floodwaters, he helped move

# Paul Bunyan of the Canadian Railway

blocks of stone, advised the carpenters on the best way to secure wooden braces, and demonstrated to blacksmiths how to make iron clamps. After saving the bridge, he retired to his private car, and soon afterward his workers heard him playing a violin solo.

Despite handsome offers from American railroads, Van Horne chose to remain in Canada, serving as president of the CPR from 1888 to 1899, then chairman until 1910. During this time he drew up plans for railroad stations, designed the interiors of the sleeping and parlor cars, and began the tradition—one that continues to the present—of hiring noted Canadian artists to decorate them with works of art.

In addition, Van Horne launched the chain of Canadian Pacific Hotels, insisting on the massive chateau style that was to influence Canadian architecture for decades. No wonder that when he died in Montreal in 1915, every CPR wheel, on every train, everywhere in Canada, stopped turning to honor him.

*Mountain Creek Bridge in the Selkirk Mountains, built in 1885 entirely of wood cut at the site, became one of the world's largest wooden edifices—164 feet high and 1,086 feet long. It required more than two million board feet of timber to span the Beaver River's valley, where mountain streams had cut deep gullies in the bare rock.*

*Luxurious Banff Springs Hotel has welcomed tourists to hot springs and Rocky Mountain splendor since 1888.*

certainly not the first traveler to make this connection. From the beginning, CPR officials followed Van Horne's scheme to "capitalize the scenery" by referring to these mountains as the "Canadian Alps."

Early railway posters and brochures drew favorable comparisons between the Rockies and the Alps and attempted to attract moneyed Europeans with promises of ultracivilized mountain resorts. A typical poster boasted of "Fifty Switzerlands in One," with Swiss guides, mountain hotels, and all the "charm and hazard of the Swiss mountains...multiplied."

Before arriving in Jasper I had discounted the alpine comparisons as typical

*Train buff passes the time in a dome car.*

travel industry hucksterism. But then I checked into the Jasper Park Lodge in time for afternoon tea on an outdoor terrace. I watched well-dressed couples gliding across a manicured lawn and children rowing across glacier blue Lac Beauvert. I read a celebrity guest list the equal of any St. Moritz hotel.

The backdrop for this luxurious setting was a characteristically Swiss one of glaciers and saw-toothed peaks with distinctive shapes. Like many European mountain resorts, Jasper was also a creation of the railroad. The frequent clanking of locomotives reminded me of Interlaken, Switzerland. I even saw some timbered and painted Hansel-and-Gretel cottages

*Late-afternoon sun glints off the Canadian's steel siding as the train rounds a bend in British Columbia.*

*Cozy quilt and pillow provide a makeshift bed for a young coach passenger.*

among the clapboard bungalows and log cabins.

Mount Edith Cavell, a snow-capped peak accessible to any reasonably outfitted day-tripper, was just 18 miles away. I drove to its base and walked to a meltwater lake afloat with miniature icebergs. The rocky face above was too sheer to hold the soft summer snows, and small avalanches cascaded with the predictability of a geyser.

When I was just about ready to swallow the "Switzerland in North America" propaganda, I passed several hiking parties heading into the backcountry. Each member had equipped himself with a bell attached to a twig. When I stopped a couple to ask why, they looked at me as if I were touched, explaining that they were relying on the faint tinkling of the bells to scare away the grizzly bears that might be lurking around the bend on even the tamest nature trail.

As if this were not enough to convince me that I had not stumbled onto some Canadian version of Gstaad, I arrived back at the Jasper Park Lodge to see waiters in white jackets riding bicycles one-handed while delivering trays of food across the sprawling grounds. They had to swerve around some elk that were wandering the grounds, devouring shrubs.

The *Canadian*'s Jasper-to-Vancouver segment packed a stunning procession of mountain wonders into its first two hours. We crossed the Continental Divide at Yellowhead Pass, among the lowest passes on the divide. The flanking mountains appeared as high as the Himalaya. We chugged in and out of avalanche tunnels, which, along with locomotives fitted with

*Engineer pilots the* Canadian *across the Fraser River.*

winged snowplows and baggage cars stocked with emergency provisions, made it possible to pass through the Rockies in winter.

For almost ten miles we had a fine view of Mount Robson, the highest peak in the Canadian Rockies. We watched the mountain darken as the sun dodged behind thin clouds, then sparkle like an iceberg when the sun reappeared, then fly a white pennant of low cumulus clouds. As the tracks twisted, passengers in the dome car swiveled their heads like tennis spectators at Wimbledon. They fell as silent as worshipers at prayer and for several minutes the only sound was the machine-gun clicking of camera shutters.

After leaving Mount Robson Provincial Park we were surrounded by clear-cuts—vast areas of surrounding slopes that had been cleared of timber. The change in scenery was as dramatic as when we left the Canadian Shield for the prairie: one moment, a thick curtain of evergreens; the next, a patchwork of clear-cuts scarring the lower slopes.

With each mile the pellucid Thompson River grew darker with soil and gravel washed from eroded slopes and logging roads. The debate over the necessity of clear-cutting as opposed to selective logging is a complicated and passionate one here. Some of the high-quality paper favored by book publishers comes from British Columbia. Acknowledging this does not make the view any more appealing, however; and I noticed that as we traveled deeper into the ravaged landscape, seats in the dome car became available for the first time since we left Jasper.

For most passengers the scarred landscape was a relatively small blemish compared to the stunning scenery of preceding days. At dinner I sat with Tom Dickey of Atlanta and his wife, Roxanne, and young daughter, Anna. For Tom, just as awesome as the views from the dome was the fact that so much wild and empty land has survived. He found it reassuring that "just when you think these kind of rugged places have vanished from the earth—here they are! Right outside the window!"

Afterward, a woman from Lexington, Kentucky, who was going to visit friends in Vancouver, told me that for her the scenery was secondary to the adventure of the journey. The trip had evoked memories of her previous rail journeys, of starched sheets, of porters collecting shoes to be polished,

and of the impeccable service she had enjoyed while traveling across the continent as a little girl to visit relatives in Oregon. "If I could travel any further than Vancouver on this train, I would," she declared. "I'm not really looking forward to getting off it."

And to be honest, neither was I. Malcolm Andrews and Paul Raynor had been right. This train *was* a comfortable cocoon, and the prospect of leaving its familiar confines suddenly seemed strangely unsettling.

The next morning I awoke to a view of red barns, orchards, and corduroy fields stretching toward snowcapped mountains, which reminded me of the evocative labels that once decorated California orange crates. Vancouver was announced by tract houses, the arches of McDonald's, a pink haze of pollution, and some misspelled

*Conductor switches the train from Canadian National to Canadian Pacific rails at Mission, British Columbia.*

*Stately evergreens abound in Vancouver's 1,000-acre Stanley Park, which opened in 1888.*

dirty words on a warehouse wall. A short taxi ride brought me to the Hotel Vancouver, another elegant railway chateau with baronial rooms, surrounded by newly erected skyscrapers.

Everything in Vancouver soared: the Hong Kong-style apartment buildings climbing hillsides, the coastal mountains rising behind the harbor, the thick forest of downtown office buildings that often doubles for Manhattan in Hollywood features, and the Teflon-coated fiberglass "sails" topping Canada Place, a convention center and cruise-ship terminal.

Contemporary facade reflects Hotel Vancouver's chateau-style copper roof, a distinctive feature of the city's skyline.

Vancouver is a city of superlatives, the perfect conclusion to my journey. It claims the world's longest and highest suspension bridge, Canada's largest urban park, the biggest port on the west coast of North America, and the highest ratio of foreign-born residents of any city on earth.

In 1994 the Corporate Resources Board of Geneva had ranked Vancouver the second best city in the world in which to live. It was certainly the cleanest, best-organized, and most beautifully situated city I have ever visited—what San Francisco would be like if it sat at the base of the Sierra Nevada.

I walked to English Bay Beach just before sunset. The horizon line was knife-sharp and beginning to flame. A procession of freighters headed out into the Pacific, their low-riding bellies loaded with wheat from Saskatchewan and timber from British Columbia. I stuck my foot in the water, recalling the moment at the beginning of my journey when I had dipped a foot in the Atlantic at history-steeped Halifax. Between Halifax and Vancouver stretch thousands of miles of tracks, knitting together this sprawling, geographically diverse country.

I realized that Tom Dickey had been right: At a time when so much empty space is being lost, a terrain so wild and vacant *has* become increasingly rare, prized, and, yes, even exotic. I knew that when I next climbed aboard a long-distance train, I would bring new memories to add to those of the *Orient Express* and the Dakar-to-Bamako local—memories of the immenseness of everything in Canada, from the Royal York Hotel to the great Rocky Mountains, and images of a landscape largely unchanged since Van Horne's laborers first laid tracks across it.

*The Steam Clock in Vancouver's Gastown, site of the city's first European settlement, puffs every quarter hour.*

**Elisabeth B. Booz,** born in London, spent many years in Asia and now lives in France and the United States. A member of the Society of Woman Geographers, she has written several books, including comprehensive guides to New Zealand and Tibet.

**Patrick R. Booz** is a freelance writer who lives in Sweden. He holds a degree in Asian Studies from the Uni-

GEORGE STEINMETZ

*Elisabeth Booz and son Patrick, who taught together in China for two years, share a pedicab and a laugh in Yibin.*

versity of Wisconsin and reports frequently on Asia, but his interest in history and geography has taken him several times to Africa. He is writing a chapter for the upcoming Special Publication *Islands Lost in Time.* **Thurston Clarke,** who lives 50 miles south of the Canadian border on Lake Champlain, is the author of *Equator* and *California Fault.* He has received numerous honors for his travel writing, including a Publication Award of the Geographic Society of Chicago and a Lowell Thomas Award. **Jodi Cobb,** a staff photographer for NATIONAL GEOGRAPHIC since 1978, has worked in more than 25 countries. She has won numerous awards, including White House Photographer of the Year, the first woman so honored. She holds Master of Arts and Bachelor of Journalism degrees from the University of Missouri. As a child, she traveled the world with her family. **Ron Fisher,** now retired after many years on the National Geographic Society staff, lives in Arlington, Va. He was born and educated in Iowa. He travels frequently— often by train but seldom so luxuriously as on the *Orient Express.* His next book for the Society, *Wild Shores of Australia,* will appear in the fall of 1996.

**Sarah Leen,** a mem-

MAGGIE STEBER

*Detail from pole shows carving skill of contemporary Haida artist Bill Reid, at the Museum of Anthropology in Vancouver.*

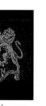

*Pullman coat of arms emblazons carpet on VSOE between London and Folkestone.*

ber of the New York photo agency Matrix, Intl., lives by the Chesapeake Bay in Edgewater, Md. She attended the University of Missouri School of Journalism. Her assignments for NATIONAL GEOGRAPHIC have included Uganda, Lake Baikal, and the American bison.

**Cynthia Russ Ramsay,** now a freelance writer based in Arlington, Va., found "the inspired architecture and engaging people make Rajasthan a fascinating destination." This assignment took her back to India, where she served as a foreign service officer before she began traveling the globe as a staff writer for the Society's Book

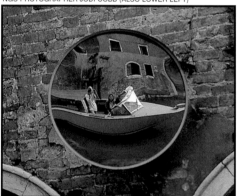

NGS PHOTOGRAPHER JODI COBB (ALSO LOWER LEFT)

*From a motorboat, Jodi Cobb snaps her own portrait in a mirror used to monitor traffic on a busy Venice canal.*

Division. **Maggie Steber** has photographed several articles for NATIONAL GEOGRAPHIC. Her book *Dancing on Fire* documents her work in Haiti. Among the honors she has received are a grant from the Alicia Patterson Foundation and the Leica Medal of Excellence. She studied photojournalism at the University of Texas.

Photographer **George Steinmetz,** a Los Angeles native, graduated from Stanford University. Assignments for the Society's books and magazines have taken him to six continents. This was his third trip to China.

SARAH LEEN

*King of beasts relaxes on the Serengeti Plain.*

# Acknowledgments

The Book Division wishes to thank the many individuals, groups, and organizations mentioned or quoted in this publication for their help and guidance.

In addition we are grateful to Lisi Adams, Embassy of Austria; Marianne Wirenfeldt Asmussen, Karen Blixen Museet; Ann Checkley, Canadian Pacific Hotels & Resorts; the crew of the VSOE; Pete D'Costa and Loretta Pinto, Travel Corporation (India) Ltd.; Guy Faulkner and Diane Graham, VIA Rail Canada; Chris Flatt, Bush Homes of East

SARAH LEEN

Door paintings in Udaipur portray the god Krishna and his beloved Radha.

Africa, Ltd.; Linda Frank, Halifax Citadel National Historic Site; Julie Fuller, Vicky Legg, and Lou Ward, Orient-Express Hotels, Ltd.; Gary R. Graves, National Museum of Natural History, Smithsonian Institution, John Israel, University of Virginia; Gabriella F. Koszorus-Varsa; John Lehnhardt, National Zoological Park, Smithsonian Institution; Colin MacKinnon, Canadian Wildlife Service; Ingrid Morejohn; Tilak Nagar; National Geographic Travel Office; Xiumin Overall; William Pierce, Brian A. Vikander Photography; Cornelia

SARAH LEEN

Ruffles and bows adorn a camel in Chittorgarh, ancient capital of a princely state in Rajasthan.

Sears; Sandra L. Sidey, National Geographic Society, France; Sumitra Singh, Embassy of India; Mustafa Siyahhan, Turkish Tourism Office; the staff of Jasper National Park; the staffs of the Canadian Railway Museum and Tourism Vancouver; Leyla Taşkim, Pera Palace Hotel; John Thibodeau, Probe International; Michael Toogood, Serengeti Balloon Safaris; Steven Varsa; Ann and Gregory Veeck, Louisiana State University; Sara Widness, Mary Homi International Public Relations.

# Additional Reading

The reader may wish to consult the *National Geographic Index* for related articles and books. The following titles may also be of interest:

**Orient Express**—Michael Barsley, *The Orient Express*; George Behrend, *Grand European Expresses*; E. H. Cookridge, *Orient Express*; Shirley Sherwood, *Venice Simplon Orient-Express*;

MAGGIE STEBER

Rearview mirror captures photographer Maggie Steber in the Canadian's engine cab on the way to Vancouver.

**East African Safari**—Bartle Bull, *Safari: A Chronicle Of Adventure*; Frans Lasson, ed., *Isak Dinesen: Her Life in Pictures*; Anna Merz, *Rhino: At the Brink of Extinction*; Charles Miller, *The Lunatic Express: An Entertainment in Imperialism*; Tepilit Ole Saitoti, *Maasai*; Sierra Club Books, *Isak Dinesen's Africa*; Judith Thurman, *Isak Dinesen: The Life of a Storyteller*;

**Rajasthan**—Charles Allen, *Lives of the Indian Princes*; Gayatri Devi and Santha Rama Rau, *A Princess Remembers: The Memoirs of the Maharani of Jaipur*; Naveen Patnaik, *A Second Paradise. Indian Courtly Life 1590-1947*; Andrew Robinson, *Maharaja: The Spectacular Heritage of Princely India*; Michael Satow & Ray Desmond, *Railways of the Raj*;

GEORGE STEINMETZ

Multilevel pavilion hugs a cliff above the Yangtze at Shibaozhai.

**Yangtze River**—Isabella Bird, *The Yangtze Valley and Beyond*; Judy Bonavia, *The Yangzi River*; May Holdsworth, *Sichuan*; Evelyn Kaye, *Amazing Traveler: Isabella Bird*; Lyman P. Van Slyke, *Yangtze: Nature, History, and the River*;

**Canada's Railroad**—Pierre Burton, *The Last Spike: The Great Railway, 1881-1885* and *The Impossible Railway*; E. J. Hart, *The Selling of Canada*; Brian D. Johnson, *Railway Country: Across Canada by Train*; W. Kaye Lamb, *History of the Canadian Pacific Railway*; Terry Pindell, *Last Train to Toronto: A Canadian Rail Odyssey*.

MAGGIE STEBER

Reflections of French countryside spangle dining car windows of a regular train following the historic route of the Orient Express.

# Index

**Boldface** indicates illustrations.

SARAH LEEN

*A painted elephant carries tourists to the fort of Amer.*

NGS PHOTOGRAPHER JODI COBB

*Live music sets a jazzy mood in the VSOE's bar car en route to Venice.*

### Library of Congress ℂℙ data

Great journeys of the world / prepared by the Book Division, National Geographic
  Society ; [contributing authors, Elisabeth B. Booz … et al. ; contributing
  photographers, Jodi Cobb … et al.].
    p.  cm.
  Includes bibliographical references and index.
  ISBN 0-7922-2942-8 (regular ed.). -- ISBN 0-7922-2972-X (deluxe ed.)
  1. Voyages and travels. I. Booz, Elisabeth Benson. II. National Geographic Society
(U.S.). Book Division.
G465.G733 1996
910.4'1--dc20                                                96--13540
                                                              ℂℙ

Composition for this book by the National Geographic Society Book Division. Printed
and bound by R. R. Donnelley & Sons, Willard, OH. Color separations by Digital Color
Image, Pennsauken, NJ; Graphic Art Service, Inc., Nashville, TN; Lanman Progressive
Co., Washington, DC; and Penn Colour Graphics, Inc., Huntingdon Valley, PA. Dust
jackets printed by Miken Companies, Inc., Cheektowaga, NY.